On Demand Writing for Students

On Demand Writing for Students

Coaching Yourself for the SAT, ACT, and AP Essays

Lynette Williamson

International Debate Education Association

New York, London & Amsterdam

Published by:
International Debate Education Association
400 West 59th Street
New York, NY 10019

Library of Congress Cataloging-in-Publication Data

Williamson, Lynette.
   On demand writing for students : coaching yourself for the SAT, ACT and AP
essays / Lynette Williamson.
       p. cm.
    ISBN 978-1-61770-027-9
  1. English language--Composition and exercises--Examinations--Study guides.
2. Exposition (Rhetoric)--Examinations--Study guides. 3. SAT (Educational
test)--Study guides. 4. ACT Assessment--Study guides. 5. Advanced placement
programs (Education)--Study guides. 6. Universities and colleges--Entrance
examinations--Study guides. I. Title.
    LB1576.W48855 2011
    808'.042076--dc23
                                             2011037494

Design by Kathleen Hayes

Printed in the USA

Contents

Preface

Forget Everything I Told You

If you want to write better on demand, the first thing you need to do is disregard everything your English teachers have taught you about the writing process. That's right—even if *I* was your English teacher—forget everything I told you.

Why?

Because writing on demand for standardized tests and holistic scoring are very different from writing an essay or a report that you can draft and revise. The limitations are numerous, and the expectations are not the same.

When You Write On Demand:

- You don't know your prompt until the writing session begins. This means little-to-no time to think. Your pen must be moving at all times—sketching an outline, jotting down examples, writing the essay.

- You don't get a second more than the allotted time. You cannot wait for a better idea, conjure the muse of perfect word choice, or run your final draft through spell-check. Your pen strokes are numbered!

- You often have to settle for less-than-spectacular examples, an oversimplified expression of an idea, or a less-than-enticing introduction. Your best writing will probably only surface occasionally, if at all.

- You will be rewarded for what you do well in constructing and developing an essay; occasional grammatical and mechanical errors will not count against you—so relax!

How This Book Helps You Write On Demand:

- It proposes ways to prepare for the different expectations of varied writing prompts.

- It instructs you on strategies for outlining, or roadmapping, essays before the actual writing begins.

- It coaches you on how to parcel out your allotted time so you can finish strong.

- It offers ways of collecting and infusing examples so you're never without specific supporting ideas for your arguments.

- It gives templates for brief but meaningful introductions and conclusions and logically developed body paragraphs.

- It provides exercises for improving sentence variety and word choice as means of climbing to the highest numbers on the scoring rubric.

How to Use This Book

On Demand Writing for Students provides sequenced lessons that can take you through the on demand writing situation from start to finish. Beginning with exercises that help you prepare examples in advance of knowing the prompt, it coaches you through prewriting, thesis construction, paragraph development, and fine-tuning sentence structure and word choice.

Each lesson begins by addressing "Why should you care?" about a particular skill and how this skill directly affects your score on standardized writing tests. Instruction then follows in the form of "What you have to know," followed by detailed steps walking you through "What you have to do." Perhaps the most beneficial portion of each lesson comes in the form of student examples. Since we sometimes learn best from seeing what not to do, the writing samples provided include not only good examples, but bad and fluffy ones as well. The good examples are to be emulated, the bad examples are blatantly awful and intended to be scoffed at, but the fluffy examples are dangerous proof that often what appears to be good writing may just be meaningless words on a page. These fluffy examples may fool those who think good writing consists of proper grammar and spelling, but they don't fool the readers of standardized writing exams, and thus should be avoided.

Accompanying the Good, Bad, and Fluffy examples is a steady stream of commentary (noted in cursive) from me. This running narrative is designed to help you discern what's effective or ineffective about a piece of writing. It's like having your very own English teacher sitting next to you marking papers with her red pen! Actually, it's a lot less painful and ideally a bit more helpful.

In addition, Chapter 8: Practice That Can Make You Nearly Perfect includes a collection of exercises designed to improve the precision of your writing. These exercises are not unique to on demand writing and may just improve your writing in general if you're not careful.

Finally, the Appendix section offers a host of references: Sample SAT and ACT prompts, responses, and scoring guides. These samples and examples offer you practice and illustrations of what works and what doesn't.

Take from This Book What Works for You and Leave the Rest

You don't have to complete all the exercises in this book and follow all the advice to improve your writing in on demand situations. Like most of my students, you will find that certain techniques click for you and others fail. No harm, no foul.

If you can already target a few areas where you struggle in on demand writing situations, feel free to seek out only those sections. Do you always have problems concluding an essay? Then flip to Lesson 17 in Chapter 5: So What? How to Write Meaningful Conclusions. Are you concerned that grammar and mechanical errors are impeding your scores? Familiarize yourself with Lesson 26 in Chapter 7: Seven Deadly Sins of Style to determine if your errors are mortally wounding your score. In other words, take what you need and leave the rest—perhaps for another time.

Ideally, this book will not only coach you through your pending on demand writing situation but also provide you with a reference that can help you get unstuck when any sort of writing is a bit too demanding.

CHAPTER 1
Planned Not Canned

One of the highest compliments that can be bestowed on public speakers is that they sound "planned not canned." This should be the goal of on demand writing as well. I want you to be prepared without having to resort to meaningless formulas.

I have learned from my students that even when the topic is an unknown variable, as in the case of standardized tests, advance preparation is still possible.

Several years ago at the state speech championships, I noticed one of my students, Julia, studying a list on a 3 x 5 card before competition. In impromptu speaking, the topics are unknown to the speaker until two minutes before the speech begins. For a brief moment, I thought Julia had gotten her hands on the topics in advance and was cheating. I half-jokingly asked if she was memorizing her next impromptu speech. To my surprise she replied, "Sort of." Then she revealed that what she had was a list of examples off the top of her head—topics that she was studying in school, books she was reading, recent films and songs, current events, etc. She explained that when she drew her topic in a round, she used the two minutes of preparation time to connect her given topic to as many subjects on her list as she could; then, she sorted the topic areas into a progressive order and constructed a "roadmap" or outline for the audience. For years, I have used Julia's "brain purge" technique to coach new impromptu speakers on my forensics team.

When the new SAT 25-minute essay debuted, I began to teach this impromptu speaking strategy to students facing on demand writing situations. What follows in this chapter are some hints and exercises to assist you with being planned not canned for on demand writing.

1. The Brain Purge: Prewriting Before the Prompt

The brain purge is a prewriting activity that creates a list of potential examples before you know the prompt. A precursor to a test or on demand writing situation, it can be done the night before.

When you don't know the topic of an essay or a speech, you often assume that you can't prepare for it. The brain purge activity offers you an opportunity to collect and focus your recent experiences into a bucket of examples that you can dip into as you organize and write the essay.

Why should you care?

Nothing is worse than the anxiety that paralyzes your brain when you're staring at an essay prompt and drawing a complete blank. "I couldn't think of anything to write about" is the most often heard refrain from students who go into a timed writing situation cold. Don't be one of them. Entering a test situation with a brain brimming with examples will give you confidence as well as plenty to write about.

What do you have to know?

Unlike a traditional essay writing experience where you are expected to brainstorm first then create multiple drafts, on demand writing is a one-shot deal. That doesn't mean, however, that you can't brainstorm—it just needs to happen before your test or on demand situation.

The object of a brain purge is to empty your head of specific details that you could use as supporting examples in an essay. Consider current events, recent films, books studied in class, personal experiences, and recent decisions. The more current the information, the more likely you are to know the nitty-gritty details and be able to flesh out the example with names, places, and dates. For instance, if you've recently had an appendectomy, you would likely be able to write about it in graphic detail, mentioning procedures and medications by name. If you had your appendix removed when you were seven years old, many of the specific facts would be hazy at best.

A brain purge is conducted before an on demand writing situation by simply grabbing a sheet of scratch paper and a pen and allowing five minutes of uninterrupted time to list everything that's on your mind without worrying about spelling or precision.

Below is a brain purge created by one of my students. As random as this list appears, it is a good, solid list of potential examples—with plenty of personal stories and opinions lurking behind each item.

Sample Purge

lack of sleep	Michael Jackson
The film *300*	cell phone bill
To Kill a Mockingbird	unfair curfew
the prom	the Vietnam War
car payment/insurance	entropy
lunch	grades
war in Iraq	baseball play-offs
Interview With the Vampire	mom's birthday
school violence	*The Simpsons*
Chris Rock	

Once you have created the list, you can begin to worry about its accuracy and precision. When I model this exercise for my students, I read over my list with them, noting that if I've forgotten the author of the book I'm reading or can't remember which Shakespearean sonnet we read yesterday, I would fact-check my information so that my list is accurate and complete before I use it to prepare for a test or an unknown prompt.

You wouldn't think of showing up for a college placement exam in chemistry without reviewing the periodic table the night before. So don't think that you can show up for an impromptu writing exam without preparing either. The more specific examples you infuse into your essay, the higher your score will climb on the rubric.

HINT

Remember the test-makers are limiting the time they give you to write *not* the time they give you to prepare!

What do you have to do?

Now it's your turn.

1. Set your stopwatch for five minutes and purge your brain by listing what's on the top of your head. List as many items as you want; the only limiting factor is the time.

   If you run dry of ideas, consider answering the following questions:
   - What was the last movie you saw?
   - Which book are you reading in English class?
   - What was the last news story you heard?
   - What are you studying in history class?
   - What are you studying in science class?
   - What's at the top of your worry list?
   - What's at the top of your to-do list?

2. Compare your brain purge with the following student samples.

The Good—Note how specific the items on the list are. Doubtless each one has a story behind it.

finding a summer job

loser boyfriend

flat tire

True Blood

Amy's birthday

cleaning closet

finding silver earring

peanut butter chocolate
     chip cookies

return band uniform

chem final

pedicure for prom

sub in fifth period

Frankenstein paper

Mrs. Gracie's tardy policy

The Bad—Note how vague this list is. In revisiting it, you may even forget what you were thinking about when you wrote "food" or "band." The great untapped story about the lost earring may be lost forever.

job

boyfriend

car

TV

birthdays

cleaning

losing stuff

food

band

chemistry

prom

paper

subs

tardies

The Fluffy—Note how the complete sentences and phrases waste ink and time to detail information the writer already knows.

finding a summer job is hard this year

my boyfriend is a bum

flat tire on my bike needs to be fixed before Saturday

True Blood is a great TV show!

Amy's birthday is this weekend

cleaning closet will get mom off my back

finding silver earring is important

peanut butter chocolate chip cookies are my #1 craving

return band uniform or die!

chem final is going to suck
pedicure for prom costs too much
Frankenstein paper on scientific ethics is due Thursday
sub in fifth period is always marking me absent
Mrs. Gracie's tardy policy has me losing credit in Spanish

Your Goal—Strike a happy medium between too much information and vague abstractions. Jot down specifics but just enough to jog your memory of events and concepts. In future brain purges, strive to avoid complete sentences and avoid single words.

3. Fact-check your list—add authors' names for the books you've listed, check the spelling on specific titles or names, and maybe include a date or two. For instance, if you've listed Amy's birthday, note how old she's turning; or, if you've included the chemistry test, indicate if it's on covalent bonding.

4. Now that you have your brain purge, it's time to make it work for you. Thumb through Appendix 1 and pick a prompt at random. Comb your brain purge list for connections to the prompt and star those items you could see connecting to a response to the prompt.

5. Set your stopwatch for five minutes and sketch out an outlined response to the prompt, folding in some of the starred examples from your brain purge.

HINT

Don't worry if you fail to use all of the starred examples or if you happen to think of a new and better example as you sketch out your outline. Consider the brain purge as a porous list—it's all right if other items seep into it.

Here's an illustration of the outlining procedure using the student brain purge above.

The Outlining Process

Brain purge:

lack of sleep	Chris Rock
the film *300*	✳ Michael Jackson
✳ *To Kill a Mockingbird*	cell phone bill
the prom	✳ unfair curfew
✳ car payment/insurance	the Vietnam War
lunch	entropy
war in Iraq	✳ grades
Interview With the Vampire	baseball play-offs
✳ school violence	mom's birthday
	The Simpsons

Prompt: Citing examples from your reading, personal experiences, and observations, agree or disagree with the premise that "justice for all" applies to teenagers.

SAMPLE OUTLINE ON JUSTICE FOR TEENAGERS

INTRODUCTION:

Personal example describing an argument with parents about Saturday's curfew

CONTROLLING IDEA OR THESIS:

Teenagers are often denied justice on issues ranging from grades to violence.

MAIN POINTS AND SUPPORTING EXAMPLES (taken from the purge!):

I. High school students are often unfairly graded

    A. grades in many subjects, such as English and art, are subjective

    B. teachers' grading policies are often unclear and inconsistent

II. In *To Kill a Mockingbird*, Mayella has no recourse against her father's abuse

    A. she was too young to be taken seriously

    B. she was too poor to garner respect

III. Many acts of school violence go unpunished

    A. hazing and harassment often go unreported

    B. punishment for reported incidents is often inconsistent

CONCLUSION (answers the questions, "Therefore what?" or "Now what?" — doesn't merely mimic the thesis):

Justice is not for all since teenagers often have no recourse when faced with unfair situations.

HINT

In constructing your outline, consider crafting your controlling idea or thesis last. Sketching out your main points and examples first is an excellent way to ensure that your thesis will, in fact, be supported by your points. When you write the essay, you can still place your thesis near the beginning.

2. Speed Prompting—Almost as Much Fun as Speed Dating!

Now that you have perfected your stopwatch technique, it's time to pare down your responses to potential prompts to just 30 seconds.

Why should you care?

When the topic of a speech or essay catches you off guard, you will often spend the bulk of your prep time mulling over your position, considering yourself lucky to conjure a single specific example. Scoring rubrics, however, reward speakers and writers for "appropriate and adequate supporting examples." In other words—they insist on multiple examples.

What do you have to know?

While the brain purge is a great way to shake out specific examples from your brain onto paper, you will also have to develop some dexterity in selecting which examples to actually use in an essay. Speed prompting, or limiting yourself to 30 seconds to connect examples to a prompt, is a great way to coach your mind to nimbly leap from topic to topic with no shortage of examples.

If you propose a topic to another student and give him only 30 seconds to agree or disagree and come up with related examples, you will simulate the on demand sensation of forcing your personal experiences and observation to fit the prompt.

While you could conduct this drill alone, the absence of an audience is likely to lessen the urgency of the on demand simulation. I recommend finding a fellow SAT sufferer and arranging a study session or meeting up online for a Facebook chat.

Below you will find sample simulations of speed prompting sessions conducted online.

The Good—In the example below, note how the responses are short but specific—very efficient. They offer just enough information for the partner to either compliment or encourage the responder to do better.

> **SAwhiz:** Agree or disagree: "Good people are good because they've come to wisdom through failure."
>
> **RUBRICator:** I disagree. My examples are: My stepbrother Frank/Phoebe from *The Catcher in the Rye*/the pitcher Tim Linsecum/Beyoncé
>
> **SAwhiz:** Not too shabby! OK give me a quote.
>
> **RUBRICator:** Here you go: "I can't give you a surefire formula for success, but I can give you a formula for failure: try to please everybody all the time."
>
> **SAwhiz:** I agree. My examples are: 4th period sub in trig/Larry my boss at pet store/ahhhh . . . that's all I got!
>
> **RUBRICator:** What about Ophelia in *Hamlet*?
>
> **SAwhiz:** Good one, thanks.
>
> **SAwhiz:** OK, your turn.

The Bad—Keeping answers too brief and too personal negates the presence of your partner. You might as well be talking or typing to yourself (which is an option, but there's less pressure and therefore less real practice of the on demand situation).

> **SAwhiz:** Agree or disagree: "Good people are good because they've come to wisdom through failure."
>
> **RUBRICator:** I disagree. My examples are: Frank/Phoebe /Tim/Beyoncé
>
> **SAwhiz:** OK, I guess . . . Now give me a quote.
>
> **RUBRICator:** Here you go: "I can't give you a surefire formula for success, but I can give you a formula for failure: try to please everybody all the time."
>
> **SAwhiz:** I agree. My examples are: The sub/Larry/ahhhh . . . that's all I got!
>
> **RUBRICator:** What about Ophelia?
>
> **SAwhiz:** Who?
>
> **RUBRICator:** Aren't you in 3rd period English?
>
> **SAwhiz:** Yes.
>
> **RUBRICator:** You know, that girl . . .
>
> **SAwhiz:** Oh, the one that sits by the window!
>
> **RUBRICator:** Never mind.

The Fluffy—If you go into too much detail, you'll nix your chances of churning out the maximum number of examples. Remember this is a prewriting exercise—you can flesh out examples in greater detail when you're actually writing the essays.

SAwhiz: Agree or disagree: "Good people are good because they've come to wisdom through failure."

RUBRICator: I disagree. My examples are: My stepbrother Frank is a really nice guy and he's pretty successful. He's got a great job and he's never had to move back in and sleep on the couch or anything. Then there's Phoebe from *The Catcher in the Rye*. She's wiser than anybody and she's never wrong. Am I out of time?

SAwhiz: YEP! Now you give me a quote.

RUBRICator: Here you go: "I can't give you a surefire formula for success, but I can give you a formula for failure: try to please everybody all the time."

SAwhiz: I agree. My examples are: 4th period sub in trig who's always trying to be our buddy. Once he even facebooked me. Larry, my boss at the pet store, is always kissing up to customers then they think he's going to give them a discount or something and when he doesn't they get pissy. This one time a lady stormed out and left her pet parakeet on the counter. What was the topic again?

RUBRICator: Failure.

SAwhiz: Right.

Your Goal—Strive to keep your examples brief but specific. Avoid abstractions, material that is too brief, and complete sentences.

HINT

On the eve of your SAT or ACT, complete a drill with 5–10 quotations. Feel your mind become more nimble as it leaps from topic to topic with a slew of examples.

What do you have to do?

To improve the rate at which you retrieve multiple examples to support a prompt, you will need a willing partner—preferably somebody who, like you, is prepping for the SATs or ACTs. Don't despair if you can't find the gumption to ask a friend to conduct this exercise in person; it could just as easily be done online while chatting on Facebook.

Before you meet, you and your partner should conduct individual brain purges. This will give you a list of examples to consult as you conduct the drill. Remember, you shouldn't limit your responses to the examples found on the brain purge—it is merely your "beginning balance"; you can and should continue to "make deposits."

You and your partner will need a stopwatch and access to a large collection of quotations. If you like, you can pick a theme for your quotations—like love, money, failure, etc. Visit a website like http://www.quotationspage.com and select a topic area. Then, randomly select a quotation and give your partner just 30 seconds to either agree or disagree and to list as many supporting examples as possible.

Remember, you're competing with yourself, not your partner. If your partner is able to sling down umpteen examples in a row, don't be discouraged, just try to beat your previous record. Working with a partner keeps you honest. You're less likely to fudge with the time limits, and you're more likely to feel the pressure of an on demand situation.

HINT

Emulate speed dating—speed prompt with a variety
of partners. Their examples may come from sources
that you hadn't considered tapping before.

CHAPTER 2
Real Writers Use Roadmaps

Whether it's done with Roman numerals or bulleted with smiley faces, there's no underestimating the importance of an outline in an on demand writing situation. On demand writing cannot grow organically—it cannot afford the time to trail off down side streets and stop for a Slurpee! It must have a destination in mind and a map that takes the writer—as well as the reader—there. In public speaking, we literally call this a "roadmap."

Debaters in a formal round of competition will preface their speeches by saying "To offer a brief roadmap, I will first address this and that, followed by my analysis of yada yada, and conclude with tah dah." Not only does this brief outline give the audience a sense of what's to come, it gives the extemporaneous speaker a map to follow in her speech. She knows the order of her ideas, and, most important, she acknowledges that everything she says must be linked to that all-important conclusion—the final argument that could win her the round.

You probably have been coached in formulaic essay writing. The five-paragraph essay formula instructs you to place the thesis of the essay first. However, this only works with a great deal of prewriting and drafting and is often forced and unnatural. For proof that theses don't always come first, consult professional editorials and columns. The theses—or essential claims—are usually found at the end of the pieces. To be sure, they have a controlling idea near the beginning, but the claim that's being proven—the crux of their argument—is scaffolded and built like a spire that reaches toward final point—of the essay. You need to first recognize this, then practice it.

3. Recognizing Roadmaps: Noting the Structure of Published Essays

When you read essays by professional writers (a.k.a. people who get paid to write essays), you'll be able to detect their roadmap skills. Their sometimes subtle overview of their main points lets you know the general ground that their piece will be covering, and, by the time you reach the destination that they've planned for you, you are also clear on their position.

Why should you care?

Reading the persuasive writing of syndicated weekly columnists is a great way to learn to appreciate and take note of varied organizational patterns for future essays all the while improving your reading skills. What's more, these writers are working within many of the same constraints as you do during an on demand writing session. They have deadlines, space limitations, and are often assigned topics of no interest to them. They may not have to perform under the shadow of a stopwatch and a scoring rubric, but their paychecks do ride on meeting deadlines and connecting with readers!

What do you have to know?

Reading short editorial pieces from your local paper is a fairly painless way to bolster your knowledge of how pros organize their essays and to possibly internalize their structure. Syndicated columns by Leonard Pitts, Maureen Dowd, Richard Cohen, Ellen Goodman, and Nicholas Kristof work well as compact pieces of writing that support a thesis and can easily be read and studied in under 20 minutes.

As you read, identify the main (controlling) idea, or thesis, and the ultimate or final argument. Note the difference between the controlling idea—the focus of the piece—and its final argument—the ultimate argument being made. For instance, a piece entitled "When a Gunshot Rings Out, Does It Make a Sound?" by syndicated columnist Leonard Pitts is a perfect example that is available on the Internet: http://www.miamiherald.com/multimedia/news/sherdavia/070706pitts.htm.

Leonard Pitts's controlling idea is America's complacency about the increase in violence against children; his ultimate argument—which appears near the end of the piece—asserts that America needs to make preventing violence against children a top priority. If Pitts were to roadmap his essay, it might look like this.

Sample Roadmap

TITLE/AUTHOR OF ESSAY:

Leonard Pitts, "When a Gunshot Rings Out, Does It Make a Sound?" (*Miami Herald*, July 7, 2006)

INTRODUCTION:

Dr. Clark's 1939 study of children and dolls lead to *Brown v. Board of Education*.

CONTROLLING IDEA OR THESIS:

America has become complacent despite the increase in violence against children.

SUPPORTING ARGUMENTS:

1. Random inner-city murders occur so frequently that they're no longer news.
    example: the recent murder of a 9-year-old girl in her front yard as she dug a grave for her doll received little press coverage

2. Death is a way of life for children in poor, violent places.
    example: children carry guns and walk past corpses on their way to school

3. This is not a black or white problem—this is an American problem.
    example: 1 in 4 persons killed in 2004 was 21 or younger

ULTIMATE ARGUMENT:

America needs to make keeping all children safe a priority.

With a couple of highlighter pens, you could easily practice following authors' roadmaps each time you read an editorial or sports column. Simply use one color of highlighter to indicate the controlling idea and ultimate argument and another color to mark the supporting examples and details. Pretty soon you'll see the pattern emerge of the controlling idea introducing the parameters of the essay in the beginning but the refined, ultimate argument being revealed near the end of the essay.

Remember, it's true what they say—the more you read, the better you'll write. What you read, however, is up to you. Don't feel guilty if you'd rather read the sports page instead of Romantic poetry. Sports writers are some of the best writers in the business. They have to employ creative strategies and refreshingly original metaphors to make someone want to read past the game stats. Hip magazines like *Rolling Stone* and *Vanity Fair* attract some of the best writers. In fact, the reading level of these magazines is higher than that of *Newsweek* or *Time*!

What do you have to do now?

Read an article on your own and trace the author's route to persuasion using the template below.

Roadmap Template

TITLE/AUTHOR OF ESSAY:

INTRODUCTION (Jot down the gist of the writer's introduction)

CONTROLLING IDEA OR THESIS (What was the writer's general position in response to an issue?):

SUPPORTING ARGUMENTS (Reasons why the writer believes his position to be valid. There's no magic number, but you should expect to find two to four reasons that will be supported with examples.):

1.

  example(s):

2.

  example(s):

3.

  example(s):

4.

  example(s):

ULTIMATE ARGUMENT: (What does the writer ultimately want us to do or to think as a result of his argument?)

HINT

Sketching out the roadmaps of professional essays reinforces the claim that real writers use roadmaps, but, most important, it will demonstrate the variety of options within a well-organized and well-written essay. Sometimes essays will have several supporting arguments, sometimes only one. Sometimes examples will be many, sometimes only a central cogent one provides support.

4. Constructing Roadmaps on Demand: Quickly Mapping Out Responses to Prompts

Being dealt a prompt and told to "plan and write an essay" in as little as 25 minutes, you may be tempted to start sprinting to the finish line, failing to realize that the secret to success is the five minutes spent mapping out the essay, not the 20 minutes spent writing it.

Why should you care?

Many of my students have admitted to writing a spectacular, compelling introduction only to look at the clock and discover that only five minutes remain to complete the essay. Nothing is worse. When you take the time to map out an essay, however, you ensure that your essay will have a destination, and you have a plan for arriving on time.

What do you have to know?

Constructing the roadmap should only take one-fifth of the total time allocated to the on demand writing prompt. For a 25-minute SAT prompt, that's 5 minutes; for a 45-minute placement test, that's 7 minutes. Then *stick to the map*! If you're halfway through writing an essay, and you get a bigger, better idea that doesn't fit your map—save it! In much the same way that you don't explore alternative routes to a job when you're late for work, on demand writing insists that arriving on time be your top priority.

As you plan your roadmap, after you've arrived at your controlling idea, determine what your ultimate argument will be, then work backward, filling out the rest of the map. One year I was fortunate to have an attorney—one of my debater's dads—address my classes on how he constructs an argument for court. He stated that he always "works backwards" from what he wants the jury or the judge to believe. If his thesis is that his client is not guilty—he knows that claiming innocence in the beginning of the argument is not as effective as providing plenty of evidence and reasons that lead logically to the ultimate argument "not guilty." This attorney's strategy may help you understand the logic behind saving the ultimate claim for the end of your essay.

The following student-generated roadmaps demonstrate three different responses to the same prompt:

Citing examples from your reading, personal experiences, and/or observations, agree or disagree with the aphorism that "Actions speak louder than words."

The Good—The good example is not only thorough but efficient in its concision. Note how the following roadmap is brief but detailed. It has very few complete sentences, yet the specific examples are ready to be elaborated on in the written essay.

Introduction: Children's nursery rhyme: "Sticks and stones may break my bones . . . "

Controlling Idea or Thesis: Words have greater influence on people than actions.

Supporting Arguments:

1. Words can incite violence or encourage peace more efficiently than actions.

    Nice, I like how you used efficiency to qualify your claim.

    example: The speeches of Martin Luther King, Jr., and Adolf Hitler

2. Words have a longer shelf life than actions.

    example: The words of great writers (e.g., Shakespeare, Orwell) continue to influence long after the author is dead.

    Effective blend of specific authors to support your point.

Ultimate Argument: While actions may have immediate impact, words are stronger tools of communication and understanding.

Good extension of your original position—you've taken your thesis somewhere meaningful!

The Bad — Note how, even though the controlling idea is strong, the supporting arguments fail to connect back to it, and the examples are far from concrete. Logical development is this roadmap's biggest flaw.

Introduction: Throughout the course of human history, countless groups and peoples have worked for change and reform through a mix of actions and words.

Referring to a specific instance would be more powerful and memorable!

Controlling Idea or Thesis: In order to have lasting impact, words must be supported by actions.

Not too shabby—you've got a nice qualified position!

Supporting Arguments:

1. In order to analyze this argument, the importance of words must first be recognized.

This statement is full of B.O. (see the end of this chapter) and it merely states the obvious—that words are important. If they weren't, there would be no point to this prompt—or, for that matter, to proving your merit by using words to write an essay!

example: Leaders who give up everything in order to provide for their people.

Do tell . . . whom do you have in mind?

2. Another aspect is the idea of diplomacy.

Another aspect of what? It's not clear if you intend to link diplomacy to your contention that words and actions work together.

example: The Civil War

Is this diplomacy?

Ultimate Argument: Words are insufficient for fulfilling people's desires and expectations, but the impact of actions is both irreversible and undeniable.

While this is a strong statement, it contradicts your original controlling idea. Instead, you should strive to take your original idea to a more specific conclusion.

The Fluffy—This roadmap has all of the makings of a solid essay, but the examples, including the one in the introduction, are too detailed and the amount of ink expended is an indication that this writer won't have enough time left to actually complete the essay!

Introduction: This one time in Miss Nguyen's 3rd grade classroom, Alex Henderson called Tim Campbell a "stupid head." Alex had to sit for a time-out during recess, but then the next day, he shoved Tim into the coat closet and that's when the entire class had to skip recess and suffer through an hour-long lesson on bullying.

> *Save the storytelling for your actual essay—remember this is a map NOT a draft!*

Controlling Idea or Thesis: Actions are powerful and have greater impact than words.

> *Clear and to the point—Bravo!*

Supporting Arguments:

1. Actions are more extreme and profound and therefore they are more memorable.

   > *A bit wordy, but it works.*

   example: One example of the power of actions is September 11th. If Osama Bin Laden had merely threatened the United States, it would have been frightening, but it would have been forgotten in a few short years. However, the organized attack on the United States was an extreme action that will remain in our memories forever.

   > *Once again, you're prewriting your body paragraphs rather than sketching a roadmap. Avoid complete sentences in your examples AND don't write out words that you can abbreviate—like United States!*

2. Actions create simple images that last longer in peoples' memory than an elaborate construction of words.

   > *Another clear supporting reason—good work!*

example: When we think of the Holocaust , we don't remember all of the words written about it, but we remember the images of starving children and burned victims. No amount of language can accurately describe an image of horror. Actions are equated with images because when we observe actions, we see visual images.

> *Great example and solid logical development, BUT with this much ink spent on mapping out your example, you won't have enough left to write your essay—remember that your map can be sketchy because you're the only one who has to be able to translate it into an essay!*

Ultimate Argument: If we want to be remembered, we must put our ideas into action.

> *Profound extension of your thesis to answer the question: What should we do or think?*

Your Goal—Strive to keep the roadmap detailed enough to prompt you to infuse examples and stay on a logical route as you write, but avoid writing out complete sentences or paragraphs.

What do you have to do?

You may begin by conducting a brain purge—but don't allow this to absorb any of the time allotted for roadmapping. Remember, the brain purge is something that should be happening outside the time constraints of the on demand essay. If this were a real test, you'd be brain purging at home before the exam.

Snag one of the retired prompts from the SAT website or select one from Appendix 1. Set the stopwatch for seven minutes and, referring to the template for a roadmap in Lesson 3, sketch out a roadmap on a piece of scratch paper.

5. Signposting: Signaling to Your Audience Where the Essay Is Going

Good roadmaps help you discover your final destination; good signposts allow you to signal to those along for the journey where they are going and why. In this case, your passengers are the readers and evaluators of your essays—so it's pretty important that they see your signs!

In a speech, the speaker is expected to "signpost" for the audience—to offer obvious indicators of where the speech is going and how the audience will get there. For example, it's very good form in a speech to state: "My first point is . . . ; my second point is . . . ; and my third and final points are . . .." This obvious phrasing in an essay signals an overly simplistic style, but with a bit of creative phrasing, the signposts can be clear as well as artful.

Why should you care?

Essay prompts are deliberately vague so as to be accessible to all. The prompts leave it up to you to narrow the scope of the discussion. An initial clear breakdown of the topic—with clear signposts—allows you to focus your essay and turn a vague topic into a potentially cogent one.

What do you have to know?

An impromptu writer can use the same signposting templates that impromptu speakers use. Generally, speakers default to one or two organizational patterns that help them organize their thoughts before they speak. Familiarize yourself with some of these templates, you're bound to find a favorite or two that will help you slice even the diciest of topics into manageable units.

Here are some common sample signposting strategies.

Signposting Strategies

Past/Present/Future: examines a topic's significance in the past compared with the present, then speculates on its role in the future.

Global/National/Local or Personal: views a topic through a broad global lens, followed by a smaller national vantage point, and concludes with a local or personal perspective.

Pros/Cons or Harms/Benefits: compares and contrasts the positive and negative aspects of a topic.

Causes/Effects: explores or speculates on the causes and effects of a topic.

Process analysis: details the steps involved in a procedure, providing opinionated analysis along the way.

Perfect world/Real world: speculates what the topic would look like in a perfect world, followed by its real-world implications.

Literal/Metaphorical (best for concrete topics): defines the common meaning of a topic, then uses it as a metaphor for a greater, more esoteric concern.

Theoretically/Pragmatically: looks at a topic as it appears in theory, then examines its practical applications.

The following student-generated roadmaps demonstrate three different signposting strategies to the prompt: Do students have free speech?

The Good—Note how this roadmap not only provides a signposted response to the prompt, it generates a position as well. Appreciate how the Good sample has also chosen a strategy well suited to the topic, allowing the writer to develop a clear position.

Signposting strategy: Real world/Perfect world

Roadmap:

- In the *real world*
  - Many high school students claim freedom of speech
    - Student newspapers and yearbooks
    - Student body elections and school board representation
  - Teachers and school administrators often curtail free speech
    - On the basis of its harmful nature
    - Out of fear of bad public relations
- In a *perfect world*
  - Students could say and write what they want—but that's unrealistic
  - The guidelines for student free speech would be clear and universally upheld

    Good! The last point is a thesis in the making; changing "would" to "should" adds the assertiveness needed to stake a claim in the conclusion of the would-be essay.

Ultimate Argument: Therefore, the guidelines for student free speech *should* be clear and universally upheld.

The Bad—This roadmap employs a signposting strategy that seems forced and is not easily supported. The prompt is asking about the current right to free speech; this strategy attempts to explore the reasons why students want it and schools don't. This could result in an essay that's grossly off topic. Experiment with a variety of signposting strategies, but be sure that the strategy fits the topic.

Signposting strategy: Causes/Effects

Roadmap:

- Causes

    - There are many reasons students want freedom of speech

    - There are many reasons why schools do not want students to have it

        > *You don't say . . . what are some of those reasons? Can you link them to the topic—student rights?*

- Effects

    - The effects of having freedom of speech are positive

    - The effects of not having freedom of speech are negative

        > *Do these negative effects impinge on student rights? If so, you may have a link to the topic!*

Ultimate Argument: Therefore, students should have freedom of speech.

> *Yikes! The ultimate argument is off topic—it fails to answer whether students have a RIGHT to free speech.*

The Fluffy—This roadmap is more detailed, and more on topic, but, while the historical perspective on freedom of speech may be interesting, it takes precious time away from exploring the essence of the question that asks—do students have (present tense verb suggests *today*!) a right to free speech? The roadmap also gives a forced and empty third point and, therefore, an insignificant conclusion.

Signposting strategy: Past/Present/Future

Roadmap:

- In the past

    - Many high school students struggled with freedom of speech

        - Students wanted to oppose wars (e.g., Vietnam) but were forbidden to protest at school

            > *This is interesting but will probably take a paragraph to explore—a paragraph that is not related to the topic of whether students have a right to free speech. You can't afford such a detour in your roadmap!*

- In the present
  - Students still struggle with freedom of speech
    - Many times newspaper articles are censored
    - Graduation speeches must first be approved by principal

      This is better, and has potential, especially if you explore WHY schools don't feel that students have the right to free speech.

- In the future
  - Students will still struggle with freedom of speech

    This is pure filler. It's an obvious statement and one that is only remotely linked to the topic.

Ultimate Argument: It will be hard, but students should not give up the fight for freedom of speech!

Why? Does it have anything to do with free speech being a right? If it's in response to this prompt, it should!

Your Goal—Consider carefully the wording of the prompt and select a signposting strategy that is efficient.

Being able to slice and dice prompts into manageable segments is a skill that instills confidence in a writer facing a surprise prompt. You will "own" the prompt after you have begun to break it down. Experimenting with a variety of signposting strategies for breaking down topics gives you ready-made patterns to plug into, allowing you to focus on the real work ahead—writing.

What do you have to do?

Experiment using a variety of the signposting strategies as you provide brief road-maps in response to the questions below, which are modeled after those found on the writing portion of the ACT exam. You don't have to respond to all the questions, but develop two or three strategies for at least four or five of them.

- Do students have a right to free speech?

- Should cell phones be banned in classrooms?

- Should the driving age be raised to 18?

- Should the voting age be lowered to 16?

- Should public service be mandatory for high school graduation?

- Is school violence on the decline?

- Should colleges expel students for plagiarism?

- Are grades a measure of student ability?

- Should attendance factor into high school graduation requirements?

6. Extemporaneous Roadmapping: Synthesizing Nonfiction Examples

Many English classes that previously focused entirely on literature—fiction and poetry—now include essays and articles. This change is, in part, attributable to the fact that many of you were at a loss for how to analyze the nonfiction pieces on the standardized exams when all you'd been asked to read were plays and short stories. This current trend to emphasize nonfiction in your English classes is echoed in the SAT's prompt stem that invites you to cite examples "from your reading." I know many of my students assumed this meant they should write about novels and stories studied in school. However, limiting examples to the literature studied in school may not be the wisest tactic. While it would be all right to mention an example from *To Kill a Mockingbird* or *Romeo and Juliet*—think of how many other students nationwide have been assigned those same books. Think of how much more original (and memorable) your examples would be if you derived them from contemporary articles and essays—and not necessarily just those you had to read for a class.

Keeping up on current events via a daily dose of Google news, a weekly news magazine, or a daily newspaper is not only worthwhile to you for conversation starters at parties, but also are likely fodder for future on demand essays as well. Adding news stories and current events to your repertoire of potential examples will make your specific supporting examples more plentiful and cogent.

What's more, you'll be practicing the art of synthesizing—the highest form of critical thinking—expected of you in college and on many Advanced Placement exams. For instance, the AP U.S. History exam offers a Document Based Question—or DBQ—where you are expected to read a collection of documents, then write an essay with an emphasis on analysis and synthesis. A few years ago, the College Board revamped its AP Language and Composition exam to include a synthesis essay—read through collected information on a topic and formulate a response to a prompt as you cite supporting evidence from the published material provided. You are allocated 20 minutes to read the provided materials and another 40 minutes to craft an essay. Since the collection of source material contains ample evidence to support either side of the proposition, I coach my students to pick their side *before* they begin reading the material. For instance, if the question were: "Is climate change having an adverse effect on the nation's economy?" the student who wants to answer "yes" should read the compiled materials, carefully selecting information that agrees that climate change is taking place and that focuses on the negative economic impacts. This "biased reading" is an efficient way of sifting through the texts for examples useful to your thesis while leaving behind the rest. This process allows you to extemporaneously—that is, with limited preparation—roadmap.

If you are college-bound, then extemporaneous roadmapping is wonderful preparation for the type of assignments you will not only encounter on AP exams like those in U.S. History and Language and Composition, but those that you will face in college-level courses. If you practice in a timed situation, these skills may help you avoid the college freshman fatality—the all-nighter.

Why should you care?

Being cognizant of current events provides you with more concrete examples to draw from when faced with the standardized prompts that invite you to cite examples from your "reading." Too often, students assume this means literature only. In this era of new skills-based standards for language arts, you are expected to read and analyze more nonfiction. This exercise in extemporaneous roadmapping not only exposes you to nonfiction, but also invites you to perform one of the highest forms of analysis—synthesis.

What do you have to know?

There's no way around it—you have to start reading more nonfiction. My students' favorite news magazine is *The Week*, a compilation of the week's best news stories. It employs several sources in crafting half-page summaries of both national and international current events in very accessible language. How do I know that this magazine is my students' favorite? It has something to do with the fact that multiple copies of the magazine are regularly "borrowed" from my classroom.

If you can't get your hands on a good glossy news magazine like *The Week*, *Newsweek*, or *Time*, then try visiting some sources online. A great quick source of controversial issues is www.procon.org. This website frames questions on current events and then offers a brief synopsis of both sides of the issue. The questions are perfect launch pads for an extemporaneous roadmap and the material is legitimate, accessible, and current.

As you thumb through your chosen material, select a news story from a particular section (e.g., national affairs) and, as you read the piece, formulate a question that could be answered by some of the information in the article. Strive to use the words "should" "could," or "would" in your question.

Here are some sample questions:

- Could peace come to the Middle East soon?
- Are organic foods healthier?
- Would life be better without cars?
- Would universal health care work in the United States?

Make it a habit to formulate would-be questions as you read articles. Even if you're reading about the outcome of last night's big game or who was nominated for a Grammy, strive to think of a question, then answer it as you read—with or without a highlighter.

Here is a sample extemporaneous roadmap sketched out by a student. He read the brief article first and formulated his own question before roadmapping his response.

THE SOURCE (author of article, title of article, name of magazine, date):
"Editor's Letter: Alone with one's self" by William Falk, *The Week*, March 27, 2009

It's a good habit to get into noting the source of your information since you may want to reference it in a timed essay to add credibility to your examples (e.g., "According to The Week magazine, social networking sites are unhealthy.")

THE QUESTION:

Are texting and social networking sites detrimental to teenage self-esteem?

YOUR ANSWER:

Yes!

REASONS *WHY* YOUR ANSWER IS CORRECT:

1. Social networking sites have more negative than positive effects on teens.
    Proof (expert quotes, facts, and examples) from the article:
    > Megan Meyer committed suicide after virtual boyfriend dumped her on myspace.

    > Cyberbullying's on the rise.

2. Text messaging degrades relationships
    Proof (expert quotes, facts, and examples) from the article:
    > Texting abbreviates conversations and makes it difficult to interpret intent or tone.

    > The endless back and forth of texting has become an addiction for an increasing number of teens.

3. These modern communications deprive their users of time better spent—alone.
    Proof (expert quotes, facts, and examples) from the article:
    > "I despise Facebook for its 'steady, Chinese-water-torture drip of status updates.' "

    > "Alone you have no choice but to make friends with yourself."

ULTIMATE ARGUMENT:

Beware of the controlling power of these devices and don't become a slave to texting and Facebook.

HINT

Feel free to also infuse examples into your
extemporaneous roadmaps that *don't* come from your
reading. Personal examples and observations are
always fair game unless you're practicing for a type
of prompt like the AP U.S. History exam's DBQ, which
instructs you to limit your information to that found
in the selected readings.

What do you have to do?

Now you're ready to scratch out an extemporaneous roadmap. Give yourself no
more than 30 minutes to do the following:

1. Secure a piece of current news from a magazine or online source.

2. After gathering the gist of the article by scanning it, craft a question about the
    topic of the article. Often the title of a news analysis piece has already done
    this for you (e.g., "Should the U.S. be worried about North Korea?" "Are M.D.'s
    Underpaid?", etc.).

3. Respond to the question simply (e.g., "Yes" or "No") or with a qualified answer
    ("Only if . . . " or "Not now, but possibly in the future . . . ").

4. Then, begin the reading looking for information that will support your position.

5. Read the article, highlighting or underlining information that pertains to your
    specific question.

6. Outline support of your answer, extracting information from the article and
    using the following template. Remember, your goal remains to beat the clock
    while keeping your map concise and on topic.

Extemporaneous Roadmapping Template

THE SOURCE (author of article, title of article, name of magazine, date):

THE QUESTION:

YOUR ANSWER (Strive for a simple response to the question [e.g., "Yes" or "No"] or a qualified answer ["Only if . . . " or "Not now, but possibly in the future . . . "]:

REASONS *WHY* YOUR ANSWER IS CORRECT:

1.

   Proof (expert quotes, facts, and examples) from the article:

   •

   •

2.

   Proof (expert quotes, facts, and examples) from the article:

   •

   •

3.

   Proof (expert quotes, facts, and examples) from the article:

   •

   •

ULTIMATE ARGUMENT: (answers the question "Therefore what?" or "Now what?"):

7. Collecting Aphorisms: Infusing Notable Quotations into Timed Essays

If you're like most people, you have an abundance of unwanted commercial jingles and pop tunes rattling around in your head. You've memorized these little ditties, but you're not proud of it. Imagine committing to memory a few quotes and mottos that you could actually use. Imagine being able to call on these memorized nuggets to sprinkle into an otherwise bland essay or to add credibility to your next on demand enterprise. Infusing notable quotations into your timed essays is an excellent way to achieve this chapter's ultimate goal of sounding planned not canned.

As a debate coach, I encourage my student speakers to latch onto catchphrases from their studies in their English and history classes and to make connections between their debate cases or impromptu topics. For example, if they are reading Shakespeare's *Macbeth*, it would serve them well to memorize the line, "Fair is foul and foul is fair" as a ready-made example of paradox that could be applied to a debate on gun control just as easily as a speech on divorce rates. Or, borrowing the line, "It's better to be feared than loved" from Machiavelli, they could offer analysis of a world leader's foreign policy or a pop celebrity's battle with the paparazzi. Not until I "caught" my speech team members employing this tactic on their timed essays did it dawn on me that students struggling with on demand writing prompts could also extract quotations from literature.

Why should you care?

Although, as Voltaire said, "A witty saying proves nothing," there's no denying that a well-placed quote can lend even the most lackluster essay a spark that qualifies as a specific detail, an essential component of a successful on demand essay. Also consider how impressive a quotation or two will be when it's discovered in a piece of writing that was composed spontaneously.

Committing a collection of quotations to memory builds a personal library of accessible aphorisms that can be employed when you're dry for an example or idea. And, who knows, having a few mottos between your ears may even afford you clever conversation at a party or picnic.

What do you have to know?

You could wait for notable quotations to stay embedded in between your ears in the same way that the annoying jingle has affixed itself; however, it will probably be more effective if you commit to collecting aphorisms in a designated place. A small notebook, a sketchbook (if you're a doodler, too), even a half-used algebra notebook will work.

Keep your notebook handy at all times—probably in the front pocket of your back-pack. When you hear a line that strikes a nerve—that makes you either wince in pain or flutter with joy—jot it down. You may encounter these mottos of meaning as you trudge through required readings for your English or social studies classes, or you may bump into some witticisms as you sit and twirl your hair during your biology teacher's lecture on cell walls. You may even stumble across a memorable line while watching a favorite film.

HINT

You could focus on a single theme as you read a work of literature in search of notable quotations or aphorisms. For instance, if you're reading *Oedipus Rex*, watch for lines that refer to truth. If *The Great Gatsby* is on your reading list, search for quotes that relate to wealth.

You will have to remind yourself to read you next assignment "actively" rather than passively. It is no longer enough for you to merely read the words—you must respond to them. Ideally, you want to leave every new book, poem, or play you read with a handful of clever quotes that can be folded into your timed essays.

You may find it frustrating to stop your reading to record the quotations for your journal, so consider reading with a pencil. When you find a quote worth saving, you can put a light pencil mark in the margin and then record the best ones later.

Since you are ultimately expected to memorize some of these lines, keep your extractions compact yet full of meaning—the very nature of a good aphorism. Consider using ellipses (. . .) if you want to record a portion of a line.

Pretending to be a student, I trolled through the list of books I teach and considered a few other poems and films that are usually explored in the senior year. What follows is my collection of lines that struck a nerve with me.

Williamson's Wit and Wisdom

"Pride grows in his heart, planted quietly but flourishing . . . until he's helpless."

King Hrothgar to Beowulf in *Beowulf*

"Seek out gold and sit on it."

The dragon to Grendel in *Grendel*

"He who fights with monsters might take care lest he become a monster."

Nietzsche quote from an anime fan in class discussion

"A man may hide an injury to his soul/But he'll never be rid of it, it's fastened forever."

from *Sir Gawain and the Green Knight*

"Since 'why' is difficult to handle, one must take refuge in 'how'."

From Toni Morrison's *The Bluest Eye*

"Let be."

Hamlet in *Hamlet*

"How dare you sport thus with life?"

the creature in Frankenstein

"There's no such thing as a true story."

Tim O'Brien in The Things They Carried

"Between the desire and the act, falls the shadow."

"The Hollow Men" by T. S. Elliot

Malcolm: "Dispute it like a man."

MacDuff: "I shall do so; But I must also feel it as a man . . . "

From Shakespeare's Macbeth

"Leave the gun, take the cannoli."

from The Godfather

Memorize *all* of these? Truth be told, I wrote this list *from* memory. That's right, all of these lines have lodged themselves between my ears—you may be surprised at the aphorisms you retain after a year of sitting in an English class! In fact, without looking at a single book, see if you can recall any one-liners from books, plays, poems, or films that you've studied over the years. You may surprise yourself!

8. Eliminating B.O.: Removing the Blatantly Obvious from Your Writing

It behooves me to inform you that I am planning to introduce to you right now a lesson that when presented will clarify to you the importance of being really, really clear when you write words that will be read.

What? Odds are that you had trouble deciphering my meaning clouded by so many unnecessary words.

Too often, student writers pad their sentences with unnecessary words in an attempt to sound impressive ("it behooves me . . . ") or to extend a limited example ("I am planning to introduce to you right now"). Regardless of the intent, the writer sounds ridiculous.

While working in a college writing lab, another teaching assistant and I struggled with a proofreading symbol for these wordy moments in student essays. Scribbling "wordy" or "redundant" seemed tedious and ineffective. That's when we devised the proofreading mark "B.O."—for "Blatantly Obvious." When students saw this in their margins—or worse yet read comments like "Your B.O. is stinking up your style!" they took notice. I use this proofreading mark to this day for its impact.

If you've ever taken a speech class or been taught how to create an effective oral argument, you may have noticed that many B.O. phrases are not only permitted, they are encouraged. Probably the most evident stylistic difference between a speech and an essay is that a speech contains blatant references to its own structure. The roadmaps are often announced—"First I will discuss . . . then I will investigate . . . " and the examples are often labeled as such—"Another example of this theory is . . . " or "This example proves that . . .." However, your writing teachers are likely to red-pencil this verbiage out of your essays as B.O.—unnecessary padding that interferes with sophisticated style.

Why should you care?

Phrases that beg the question or pad an answer are unnecessary and detract from the impact or urgency of a statement. "It feels to me as if students should be given greater freedom of speech on campus" softens the impact of asserting, "Students should be given greater freedom of speech on campus."

If you are interested in reaching the upper end of the scoring rubrics, you need to heed stylistic choices as well as structural ones. I've yet to read a high-end essay released by the College Board that features redundancy and B.O. In fact, every year, I challenge my students: if they can find a professional columnist who uses the phrase "in conclusion," I will award them extra credit. To date, I've had to dole out one portion of extra credit—to a sly student who inserted the line into his own weekly column for the local paper.

What do you have to know?

The simplest ways to avoid B.O. are to read professional writers' work and review your own. Note how infrequently, if at all, you find any of these B.O. phrases in a published piece:

B.O. (Blatantly Obvious) Phrases That Stink Up Your Writing

"I feel . . . "

"I think . . . "

"I believe . . . "

"I will show . . . "

"In this essay . . . "

"In my opinion . . . "

"I agree/disagree . . . "

"It seems to me that . . . "

"In conclusion . . . "

"We will examine . . . "

"I have proven that . . . "

"Another example is . . . "

"This is true/false for three reasons . . . "

Scrutinize a piece of your old writing to determine which B.O. phrases creep into your writing most often. I once had a student who couldn't wean himself from the phrase "I believe." One day I read aloud one of his papers on *Macbeth*, and I loudly emphasized every "I believe" as if I were a Southern preacher—complete with fist pumps into the air. Laughing and shaking his head in disbelief, the student pleaded, "Stop it—you sound ridiculous!" He couldn't have been more right.

HINT

Students frequently ask me "How will the reader know that this is my opinion if I don't say that it is?" To which I reply, "Who else would the opinion belong to? You wrote the essay; you own the ideas."

Once you've determined which bits of B.O. frequent your prose, create a short list of your stinky phrases and set out to eradicate them from your writing.

If you heeded the signposting strategies explained in Chapter Five, you may run the risk of sounding blatantly obvious in your phrasing when you actually write the essay. To observe how to artfully dodge the B.O. in a signposted essay, note the following Good, Bad, and Fluffy introductory paragraphs that employ the signposting strategy of pros and cons.

The Good

Free speech for high school students has its pros and cons. When high school students are granted free speech, they are given a voice in their school, which can foster respect among the faculty and other adults on campus. However, if that voice is not fact-checked, the student may cause permanent harm to others if falsehoods are presented as facts are broadcast or printed.

This introduction relies on the signposting strategy of pros and cons, but, after the first sentence, it trusts its phrasing *to convey which reasons are pros and which are cons. The style is artful and compact.*

The Bad

There are many pros and cons to free speech for high school students. One pro is high school students being given a voice in their school. Another pro is the respect that this voice can foster among the faculty. Some of the cons include the school's liability for slanderous things a student may say or write and the permanent damage that can result when a student publication prints incorrect information.

This introduction utilizes the signposting strategy of pros and cons, but unnecessarily draws attention to the terms "pro" and "con" even when it's blatantly obvious which reasons are which. In repeating the signposts, the writer also creates awkward phrasing (e.g., "Another pro is . . . ").

The Fluffy

Free speech for high school students has its pros and cons. One positive benefit of high school students being granted free speech is that their voice in the school becomes louder and this can create another plus which is faculty and other adults on campus respecting the students more. A potentially negative side effect of students having free speech is the permanent harm the students can cause if false information is broadcast or printed.

This introduction attempts to eliminate the blatantly obvious phrasing by finding replacements for the terms "pro" and "con." This results in a wordy convoluted syntax that muddles meaning.

Your Goal—When I am bombarded by B.O in student writing, I tell my students that good writing is like sniper fire—it hits its target with precision. B.O. is more like a shotgun blast of words that may or may not graze the target. Ready, aim, *fire*! . . . with accuracy.

What do you have to do?

Test your B.O. sensors and challenge yourself to eradicate all of the B.O. in the following mini-essay.

Do students have a right to free speech? In this essay I will show that there is a difference between free speech for students in the real world and in a perfect world.

In the real world, many high school students claim to have freedom of speech. Students publish their views in on-campus publications like student-run newspapers and yearbook publications. Another example is when students represent the student body as officers or as school board representatives. I think that these positions give students a voice in how the school is run, but I don't agree that these opportunities necessarily grant students free speech.

Teachers and school administrators often curtail freedom of speech. When principals and teachers find student expression potentially harmful, I feel that they must intervene. For example, if a student wears a T-shirt advertising beer or making a racial slur, I agree that the school should squelch the speech. Sometimes a school will react negatively to student speech if it expresses something that may be bad for the school's public relations. For example, if there are lousy leaky bathrooms on campus, the school may be struggling to fix them and not appreciate a student's editorial column critiquing the quality of the bathrooms on campus.

In a perfect world, students could say and write what they want. Perhaps a more realistic model of perfection, however, would be one in which the guidelines for student free speech would be clear and universally upheld. If students were clear about the limits of their free speech, they would be less likely to breach the restrictions and more likely to express themselves within the guidelines. If the consequences for hurtful speech were the same from campus to campus, then students would have a greater sense of fairness and feel less threatened by limits on their free speech.

In conclusion, the guidelines for student free speech should be clear to all students and universally upheld by school administrators.

Here is same student sample essay after being scoured for B.O. and attacked by my red pen.

Do students have a right to free speech? ~~In this essay I will show that~~ *(this is obviously an essay and you are expected to show us something!)* There is a difference between free speech for students in the real world and in a perfect world.

In the real world, many high school students claim to have freedom of speech. Students publish their views in on-campus publications like student-run newspapers and yearbook publications. ~~Another example is when~~ *(Not only is it unnecessary to refer to an example as an example, but the phrase "another example of this is . . ." sets you up for awkward syntax!)* **When** students represent the student body as officers or as school board representatives, ~~I think that~~ these positions give students a voice in how the school is run, but ~~I don't agree that~~ these opportunities **don't** necessarily grant students free speech.

Teachers and school administrators often curtail freedom of speech. When principals and teachers find student expression potentially harmful, ~~I feel that~~ *Often students insert phrases like " I feel" to soften the emphatic nature of their argument or to avoid a sweeping generalization. Both of these goals can be accomplished by replacing the word "must" with "should" as follows.* they ~~must~~ **should** intervene. For example, *While not necessary, a single "for example" may help you transition, however, with another "for example" echoing later in the same paragraph, you risk bogging down your essay in redundancy.* if a student wears a T-shirt advertising beer or making a racial slur, ~~I agree that~~ the school should squelch the speech. Sometimes a school will react negatively to student speech if it expresses something that may be bad for the school's public relations. ~~For example,~~ If there are lousy leaky bathrooms on campus, the school may be struggling to fix them and not appreciate a student's editorial column critiquing the quality of the bathrooms on campus.

In a perfect world, students could say and write what they want. Perhaps a more realistic model of perfection, however, would be one in which the guidelines for student free speech would be clear and universally upheld. If students were clear about the limits of their free speech, they would be less likely to breach the restrictions and more likely to express themselves within the guidelines. If the consequences for hurtful speech were the same from campus to campus, then students would have a greater sense of fairness and feel less threatened by limits on their free speech.

~~In conclusion,~~ Instead of stating the obvious "in conclusion," address WHY your conclusion is a good idea or what it solves for. **To insure mutual respect for freedom of expression**, the guidelines for student free speech should be clear to all students and universally upheld by school administrators.

CHAPTER 3
Thinking Inductively, Writing Deductively

Our brains take in specific information and through induction draw conclusions.

When you were little, you probably put something icky onto your mouth. Whether it was a green strawberry or one of the dog's chew toys, your powers of induction concluded that those things were not tasty, and, odds are, you never snacked on unripe strawberries or Fido's rawhide bone again.

Inductive thinking allows us to make connections—to make sense of our world. When we're trying to persuade someone of our findings, however, we reverse these organic processes and begin with a general premise (e.g., Don't eat that—it belongs to the dog!). Beginning with a general premise and moving toward specific supporting examples is known as deductive reasoning; it is more sophisticated than induction and relies on artful construction.

Deduction is a complicated and often unnatural procedure for beginning writers. Most young students are apt to simply record their inductive thought processes without giving consideration to converting their ideas into a persuasive, deductively arranged argument. If, for instance, a child in third grade is reading a book and every time the character named "Peter" appears he acts selfishly, the student may inductively arrive at the claim: the character Peter is selfish. When asked to write a character analysis of Peter, the student may simply present a series of examples of Peter acting selfishly without making a claim about Peter's selfishness. I call this the "clothesline essay"—a series of examples strung together without developing an argument (e.g., Peter acts selfishly in Chapter Three. Another example of Peter acting selfishly comes at the end of the book, etc.). By the time the student reaches high school, teachers—or anyone reading the student's essay—would expect the essay to stake a claim, then support it with examples from the book. (e.g., Peter acts selfishly as a defense mechanism. This is illustrated in Chapter Three when . . .).

To help you develop your ideas logically and avoid the "clothesline essay," this chapter has practice exercises to help you recognize the difference between inductive and deductive thinking, then it will assist you in discovering how you typically organize your thoughts when faced with a particular prompt. For instance, given the prompt "Is it good to be selfish?," you may immediately respond with a general premise and deductively declare: "No, it is never a positive attribute to be selfish." Or, you might reply with a specific example and inductively reason: "My brother Peter was very selfish toward me when I was little, but his unwillingness to share increased my self-reliance and independence." Once you can recognize your inductive and deductive patterns of thought, you are more likely to be able to effectively manipulate the order of ideas for a formal essay.

9. Brain Lather: Quick Writing to Diagnose Inductive or Deductive Thinking

When I first assigned this exercise, I told my students that they were going to have an opportunity to blather on paper for seven minutes. When one student asked what I meant by "blather," another student replied that it sounded like "brain lather"—a metaphoric foaming at the brain. His description captured the essence of a quick write—to pen thoughts without attention to mechanics or structure. This spontaneous writing is probably the best method for you to discover how your brain constructs arguments naturally. Understanding this natural process is the first step in manipulating your thinking for on demand writing situations.

Why should you care?

Most students have been well trained since grade school to put a topic sentence at the beginning of a paragraph and to tuck in the concrete examples below it. What you may not have been taught, however, is that this deductive reasoning can only come after you have formulated arguments inductively. This exercise will help you see this organic process and guide you toward manipulating it for on demand writing situations.

When a piece of writing is holistically scored, the evaluator can easily skim the essay's content if the body paragraphs begin with clear claims. Paragraphs that begin with an assertion like "Money is more important than love" score points for critical thinking, whereas paragraphs that begin with "Another example of money's importance to love is when . . . " lose points for lackluster reasoning as well as awkward syntax.

What do you have to know?

Making sense of the world requires logic. Even earliest man employed logic to arrive at conclusions about his universe. When stepping on something sharp hurt or when eating something resulted in a stomachache, our powers of logic allowed us to make connections, draw conclusions, and ideally warn others of the potential consequences. Our reasoning capabilities consist of two types: inductive and deductive. Inductive can lead to deductive as illustrated below.

Types of Reasoning

Inductive Reasoning—going from the specific to the general—is the most common and primitive type of reasoning. For example:

evidence	Org ate the red plant and died that night.
	Ugh ate the red plant and died that night.
	Ick ate the red plant and died that night.
assertion	The red plant killed them.
conclusion	The red plant is deadly.

Sometimes—if we're smart or lucky—induction leads to deduction.

Deductive Reasoning—goes from the general to the specific. For example:

major premise	The red plant is deadly.
minor premise	Ur ate the red plant.
conclusion	Ur will die.

Writers use both inductive and deductive reasoning to express their ideas. See if you can determine which of the following paragraphs is inductive and which is deductive.

Prompt: Are grades an accurate measure of students' abilities?

Paragraph 1: Every once in a while there's a boy in history class who knows everything about the trade routes of Russia, but when test time comes around Joe Schmart scores a "D" while the class averages an 85. School smarts are completely different from a student's true potential and talent. Grades fairly assess someone's talent only if he or she is committed to playing the game of being a good student.

Is the above paragraph inductive or deductive? That's right, it's inductive; it moves from a specific example about the boy in history class and toward the general claim that grades only fairly assess talent if the student is committed to playing the game.

Paragraph 2: Students who are very intelligent and who have high potential might receive poor grades. Grades factor in punctuality, neatness, and ability to work under pressure, often measuring a student's performance rather than intellect. My neighbor receives Cs yet he scored a 2200 on his SATs; I studied for four months for my SATs and barely scored a 1700, yet I maintain a 4.0 GPA at school.

Is the above paragraph inductive or deductive? It's deductive; it moves from a general claim asserting that intelligent students can receive poor grades. It then goes on to prove the claim with examples and reasons why grades measure performance, not intellect.

You may have noticed that both of the above paragraphs are well written. *So* you may be asking yourself, "Why can't I write inductively in a timed essay?" Well, you can, but the deductively constructed paragraph is easier to scan and indicates clear organization to the evaluator. Don't forget, on the SAT or the ACT test, you are actually persuading the evaluator to accept your argument; this requires making claims first, then offering supporting data to tell the reader what to make of the examples. Otherwise your examples run the risk of being lost before the claim can be made.

Remember, early man, just like young children, learned inductively but then shared that knowledge deductively with those less experienced. A lifeguard who barks "Walk, don't run!" at children cavorting around a pool didn't need to fall and crack her skull to know that running around a concrete pool could lead to injury. She's capable of making her argument deductively, and so are you.

What do you have to do?

To discover how your brain is hardwired—that is to say whether you automatically default to inductive or deductive reasoning when you face a writing prompt—follow these simple steps:

1. Set the timer for seven minutes and quick write a response to one of the following prompts:

    •   Are grades an accurate measure of students' abilities?

    •   Are cell phones a distraction in the classroom?

    •   Do spirit rallies improve student morale?

Keep your pen or pencil flowing across the page for the full seven minutes—there is no need to pause to correct errors or to think of precisely the right word.

2. After the seven minutes have elapsed, read what you wrote and underline any concrete detail or specific examples.

    •   If you have concrete detail or specific examples in your first two sentences, draw a triangle on the top of your paper. The tip of the triangle represents specific examples while the base of the triangle represents the general conclusions being drawn.

    •   If you don't have concrete detail or specific examples in your first two sentences, draw an upside down triangle on your paper. This indicates that your general claims were made first and that specific examples—the tip of the triangle—will follow to support the claims.

Neither triangle is a badge of shame or honor but merely denotes a difference in the way you constructed your argument. The upright triangle represents inductive thinking, while the inverted triangle suggests deductive reasoning. If you discovered that you are an inductive thinker, you must concentrate on reversing your natural structure when constructing a formal argument for an essay. If you responded naturally with a general claim, then you are on your way to constructing a deductively reasoned argument, but you may need to coax yourself into remembering to always provide concrete specific supporting examples as well.

10. Data/Warrant/Claim: Transforming Inductive Thinking into Deductive Writing

When I log onto my school's attendance program, a student who is legitimately absent because of illness or a school activity will be designated by a "W" for a "Warranted absence." That student is spared my wrath because he had a valid reason for missing my class. Essays without warrants are like unwarranted absences—they raise all sorts of questions and leave your words vulnerable to interpretation.

When you were first introduced to the brain purge exercise in Chapter One, you were collecting potential examples for use in an essay. The examples, or data, were assembled first, then the prompt was distributed, and bits of data were selected that would help support your response to the prompt. For instance, you may have noted on your brain purge a recent hallway incident where a group of seniors deliberately tripped a freshman. When you were given the topic of teenage justice, you selected this example from your brain purge and then reasoned that many acts of school violence go unpunished because they are never reported by the intimidated victims. This very primitive procedure follows philosopher Stephen Toulmin's model for inductive reasoning—data (evidence), warrant (analysis), and claim (thesis).

> **Data:** group of seniors deliberately tripped a freshman in the hall
> **Warrant:** since the victim of the violence was intimidated by the seniors, he did not report the incident
> **Claim:** Therefore, many acts of school violence go unpunished since they are often unreported

The claim, or thesis, is drawn at the end of data collection and analysis. However, as we now know, most formal arguments—whether in the form of a court case or the body paragraphs of an essay—begin with general statements followed by supporting details.

HINT

Why should you care?

Identifying data, warrants, and claims is the first step in making certain that each essay you construct has all three essential elements of an argument.

Discerning an opinion or assertion from a fact or bit of data is essential not only for writers, but for readers as well. This distinction is a frequent question on the reading portion of standardized tests.

Warrantless claims are illogical and fail to earn points for critical thinking, while a string of examples without warrants linking them to a claim is meaningless and ineffective. Therefore, understanding how the components of data, warrant, and claim operate in an essay is a critical step in controlling these elements to your advantage in on demand writing.

What do you have to know?

Deciphering data from warrants and claims is fairly simple. Being able to ensure that your warrants and claims are clearly linked, however, is more of a challenge.

Consider the following chart in which students were given data, then asked to write appropriate warrants and claims from the data. You'll note that in the Good student samples, a very clear link is present between the warrant and the claim. These links have been underlined so you can appreciate their overlap.

Data (the facts)	Warrant (reason why you think the data are true or significant)	Claim (what—if anything—should be done about the data and the warrant)
In 2003, only 34% of high school seniors reported studying or doing homework 6 or more hours per week; in 1987, 47% of students studied at least 6 hours weekly.	**Good** High school curriculum is getting less <u>intense</u>. **Bad** Kids have gotten lazy.	**Good** <u>Intensify</u> the curriculum. **Bad** Students should wake up and smell the coffee! *This claim is not linked to the warrant. There's no reason offered why kids need to wake up!*
In America, 7 billion gallons of water are used daily on residential lawns.	**Good** Americans waste water on <u>nonessential</u> uses. **Fluffy** Americans waste water.	**Good** Ration the amount of water that Americans can use for <u>nonessential</u> purposes. **Fluffy** Americans don't conserve water. *This statement begs the question and repeats the warrant in different terms without making a claim of what we should do about the problem.*
In 2006, sales of dolls, action figures, and outdoor toys were down sharply, while electronic sales to children were up 16.6%.	**Good** The rise of <u>technology</u> has created new demands for electronic <u>toys</u>. **Bad** Kids only want electronic toys.	**Good** <u>Toy</u> companies should invest more in processor chip <u>technology</u>. **Bad** Kids have been brainwashed. *There is a missing link here! How did we get from what kids want to their being brainwashed?*

Data	Warrant	Claim
Forty-seven percent of dogs in the U.S. are permitted to sleep in a family member's bed.	**Good** American families treat their pets like <u>members</u> of the <u>family</u>. **Fluffy** Dogs have gotten lonelier. *There is no evidence for this warrant—making the claim that follows ridiculous as well.*	**Good** Pet accessory manufacturers should appeal to <u>parenting</u> instincts and market their products using guilt. **Fluffy** Dogs need to sleep with their owners.
In 2001, spam accounted for 5% of Internet traffic; today it's often 90%—more than 100 billion unsolicited messages every day.	**Good** The <u>profitability</u> from <u>spam</u> is increasing, drawing in more respondents. **Bad** As the Internet becomes more popular, scam artists are trying to cash in on it.	**Good** Internet users should <u>invest</u> in good <u>spam</u> filters to avoid the <u>expense</u> of being scammed. **Bad** There are more scams online. *This observation—which may or may not be true—is not a claim. It doesn't tell us what to do or think about the warrant.*
Nationally, only 46% of people summoned for jury duty actually show up.	**Good** Americans are not taking their <u>civic obligation</u> of <u>jury duty</u> seriously. **Fluffy** The majority of Americans ignore their civic duties. *First of all, the data doesn't support this—46% is not a majority.*	**Good** Americans who fail to respond for <u>jury duty</u> should be made to attend a class on <u>civic responsibility</u> and/or fined. **Fluffy** Americans prefer to be lawless anarchists. *Huh? How did we get from ignoring civic duty to a revolution?*

Ultimately, these logical units need to be organized into paragraphs so they can form the body of an essay. When converting data, warrant, claim into a paragraph, the arrangement of the elements becomes:

Warrant

Data

Claim

Here is a sample paragraph that uses the warrant (**w**), data (**d**), and claim (**c**) from the first item on the sample grid.

The high school curriculum is getting less intense (**w**). In 2003, only 34% of high school seniors reported studying or doing homework 6 or more hours per week; whereas, in 1987, 47% of students studied at least 6 hours weekly (**d**). To ready students for the rigors of college, high school curriculum should be intensified (**c**).

What do you have to do?

Complete the following grid by supplying new warrants and claims for the data given above. There are no right answers! In fact, you should be able to conceive of multiple warrants and claims for each piece of data.

Data (the facts)	Warrant (reason why you think the data are true or significant)	Claim (what—if anything—should be done about the data and the warrant)
In 2003, only 34% of high school seniors reported studying or doing homework 6 or more hours per week; in 1987, 47% of students studied at least 6 hours weekly.		

Data	Warrant	Claim
In America, 7 billion gallons of water are used daily on residential lawns.		
In 2006, sales of dolls, action figures, and outdoor toys were down sharply, while electronic sales to children were up 16.6%.		
Forty-seven percent of dogs in the U.S. are permitted to sleep in a family member's bed.		
In 2001, spam accounted for 5% of internet traffic; today it's often 90%—more than 100 billion unsolicited messages every day.		
Nationally, only 46% of people summoned for jury duty actually show up.		

Working with the information supplied in the above table, extract data, warrant, and claim for one of the topic areas. Then, rearrange the information into a paragraph that puts the warrant first, then the data, followed by the claim.

11. Double Data: Using the Same Evidence to Support Opposing Claims

As you discovered in the previous lesson, you can assert radically different claims based on the same data. For example, given the data that in 2003 a record 46.6% of college-bound seniors earned "A" grades compared with a record low of 17.6% in 1968 you could claim—"Teachers are inflating grades" or " Students are working harder." Data don't make an argument by themselves—that takes reasoning. To test your powers of reasoning, we are going to experiment with using the same bit of data to prove opposing claims.

Why should you care?

On the writing portion of the ACT exam and many placement exams, the writing prompt includes an article or brief blurb of information, then the prompt invites you to agree or disagree with a claim. The information or article is designed to help you support either position. The test-makers aren't giving you a position, they're giving you the data to support a position—and they anticipate that opinions will vary.

What do you have to know?

Many times in an on demand writing situation, you may be faced with a prompt that asks you to agree or disagree with a position that you don't even care about—one on which you don't have an opinion at all. Your toughest challenge may be determining which position to support and to do so consistently and with compelling arguments. Even if it's a small anecdotal example, an essay with personal buy-in has greater potential for persuasive power than a logically sound but bland paper.

If, for instance, you are not a particularly stressed person, and you were asked by an on demand prompt to argue whether small amounts of stress are good or bad for students—you may not care. If the prompt provided you with a recent study that showed that short-term stressors can be good for your health, you still may think, OK, but so what? With a bit of reasoning, however, you could conceivably use this little bit of data to support an argument in favor of more short-term stress for teens or one in which you called for stress reduction.

> According to a study published in the American Psychological Association's *Psychological Bulletin* in July 2004, short-term stressors—like SATs or the bar exam—appear to boost Th2 cells that produce antibodies and worsen allergies, but help to fight the early stages of infection.

Here is a sample, using the data above, that argues that taking the SAT is *good* for your health. (The use of data is underlined.)

> Despite the bad rap that society tends to give to stress, it can actually help protect our bodies from harm. <u>One study revealed that when subjected to short-term stressors—like SATs or the bar exam—test subjects' fast-acting immune responses were triggered, jump-starting their bodies' all-purpose defense systems for fending off infection and healing wounds.</u> Teachers should incorporate more unexpected, immediate exercises into their lesson plans. This will help boost students' immune systems, as well as test how much knowledge they actually absorb in class.

Using the same data, you can argue that taking the SAT is *bad* for your health.

> Stressful situations not only create a sense of distress in most victims but may actually harm their health as well. <u>When test subjects in a recent study were subjected to short-term stressors—like SATs or the bar exam—test subjects' fast-acting immune responses were triggered, jump-starting their bodies' all-purpose defense systems for fending off infection and healing wounds.</u> If the immune systems of the stressed are boosted, they may avoid otherwise nasty afflictions to their health such as colds and flu. Without these ailments, they will visit their health care providers less frequently, possibly leaving less symptomatic but more life-threatening illnesses like cancer or heart disease to fester and worsen. Therefore, the short-term benefits of stress on the body do not outweigh the harmful impacts.

What do you have to do?

To gain flexibility in your reasoning skills, experiment with using the data below to support opposing claims.

Data: In 2010, 41 percent of new college grads turned down job offers.

Use the data to argue: Current college grads are picky and lazy.

Use the same data to argue: Current college grads are struggling to find jobs worthy of their degrees.

Data: A child born into a home with 500 or more books will, on average, attain three years more of formal education than a child with no books at home.

Use the data to argue: Keeping books in the house is essential for raising smart kids.

Use the same data to argue: Keeping books in the house will increase a family's college spending.

Data: Economists calculated that every dollar invested in preschool for at-risk kids brings an $8–9 return to society.

Use the data to argue: Governments need to invest more in preschool for at-risk kids.

Use the same data to argue: Preschool should be mandatory.

CHAPTER 4
Understanding Prompts from the Inside Out

Part of the anxiety clouding the on demand writing experience is the unpredictable prompts that remain a mystery until the clock starts ticking. While you can't predict the precise topics addressed by the prompts, you can decipher the expectations of various types of prompts and coach yourself to recognize them.

- Does the prompt want me to tell a story?
- Does it want me to use examples from a selected piece of reading?
- Does it want me to argue a point?
- Am I expected to evaluate an argument?

The more comfortable you become with different types of prompts and their formulaic nature, the better you will be able to meet the expectations of the test.

One of the best ways to familiarize yourself with the specific expectations of various prompts is to analyze professionally written prompts in order to craft some of your own. Of course, you'll be cordially invited to then practice responding to these prompts.

In this chapter, you'll be encouraged to think like a teacher (a frightening prospect, to be sure!) and to generate your own writing prompts, then you'll be coached and cajoled into responding to prompts with a qualified thesis statement—guaranteed to both strengthen your critical thinking and improve your organization. Finally, you'll be given a take-it or leave-it strategy for dealing with abstract prompts. Ideally,

you'll discover that the more control you exert on these vague prompts, the more

focused and meaningful your responses will be.

12. The Prompt Generator: Student-generated Prompts

The best way to dispel fear is to participate in the experience. Afraid of haunted houses? Don a gory mask and jump out from behind a curtain at the next Halloween party. Afraid of the types of questions that might appear on a tough biology final? Try anticipating what your teacher will put on the test and write a few sample questions.

Emulating the prompts that appear on standardized tests can dispel their mystery, make them more familiar, and, therefore, more accessible to you. By investigating sample prompts or retired tests for the particular exam you'll be taking, you can extract the predictable prompt stem and determine how best to structure your response. For instance, after imitating a series of prompts that begin with the stem "Confirm, challenge, or qualify the following assertion . . . ," you will begin to recognize an invitation to write a persuasive essay. After the third or fourth attempt at writing a prompt that begins with the stem "Describe a time when . . . ," you'll be able to identify the opportunity to respond with a narrative essay.

Why should you care?

When an essay fails to address a prompt, it qualifies for the lowest score on the rubric. Often well-written, creative essays are assigned to the low end of the scoring scale because they failed to address *all* parts of a prompt or because they told a story when they were expected to construct an argument. Recently one of my students wrote an incredibly detailed, interesting essay in which she argued *how* "fiction is an effective vehicle for truth" in Tim O'Brien's *The Things They Carried*. Unfortunately, the prompt stem had asked her to *evaluate* if "fiction is an effective vehicle for truth." This was a major mistake, and several pained peer-evaluators came to me with her essay and the same question on their lips: "Do I have to give this essay a low score? It's off topic, but it's so well written." To which I had no choice but to reply, "You can note that, right below the '1' that off-topic essays must receive."

Although it may seem superficial, writing some of your own prompts will force you to consciously acknowledge each element of the prompt and allow you to understand the test-maker's intent from the inside out. Most important, you'll become too savvy to ever write an off-topic essay.

What do you have to know?

Writing prompts consist of two distinct elements: the specific topic and the prompt stem. The topic (e.g., family traditions, free speech, fear, etc.) varies for each prompt. The prompt stem, on the other hand, essentially remains the same for a particular test. For instance, the AP Language Composition open question routinely invites students to "confirm, challenge, or qualify" an assertion; the SAT reasoning test, however, insists that writers "agree or disagree with the ideas expressed in the above quotation."

Familiarizing yourself with the type of prompts you'll be facing on the test is critical. Visit the websites for the tests and you'll find retired tests and former prompts. As you read over the previous prompts, a pattern should emerge. Let's analyze sample prompts featured on four different types of standardized writing tests. The prompt stems, whose style is unique to each type of test, are underlined.

Sample Prompts

SAT PROMPT (from www.collegeboard.com)

Quotation: "A society composed of men and women who are not bound by convention—in other words, they do not act according to what others say or do—is far more lively than one in which all people behave alike. When each person's character is developed individually and differences of opinion are acceptable, it is beneficial to interact with new people because they are not mere replicas of those whom one has already met."

Adapted from Bertrand Russell, *The Conquest of Happiness*

Prompt: Is it better for a society when people act as individuals rather than copying the ideas and opinions of others? <u>Plan and write an essay in which you</u>

develop your point of view on this issue. Support your position with reasoning and examples taken from your reading, studies, experience, or observations.

Analysis: Notice how the prompt offers a summary of the quotation in the form of a question: "Is it better for a society when people act as individuals rather than copying the ideas and opinions of others?" You should first answer the question, yes or no, then determine your supporting examples and reasons. With this style of prompt in the form of a question, students often fear that there is a correct answer. There isn't. Rest assured that the test-makers selected the quotation and the topic because it was debatable. The readers are interested in how well you construct an argument in favor or against the proposition, so you should pick the side that you could best support with lush examples and solid reasoning.

ACT PROMPT (from www.actstudent.org)

Issue: Educators debate extending high school to five years because of increasing demands on students from employers and colleges to participate in extracurricular activities and community service in addition to having high grades. Some educators support extending high school to five years because they think students need more time to achieve all that is expected of them. Other educators oppose the extension because they think students would lose interest in school and attendance would drop in the fifth year. In your opinion, should high school be extended to five years?

Prompt: In your essay, take a position on this question. You may write about either one of the two points of view given, or you may present a different point of view on this question. Use specific reasons and examples to support your position.

Analysis: Unlike the SAT prompt stem, which gave you the option of saying yes or no, this prompt stem gives you a third option: "present a different point of view." While it's perfectly legitimate to support extending high school to five years or arguing that this would be a bad idea, it is also permissible to present an alternative plan such as shortening the high school term to three years or mandating that the fifth year be spent fulfilling a national service requirement. It's crucial that you are able to detect when the prompts are inviting a creative alternative and when they simply want you to agree or disagree. Remember, straying from the prompt's directions is grounds for the lowest score on the rubric—no matter how well written your essay.

AP LANGUAGE & COMPOSITION PROMPT (from www. apcentral.collegeboard.com)

Issue: For years corporations have sponsored high school sports. Their ads are found on the outfield fence at baseball parks or on the walls of the gymnasium, the football stadium, or even the locker room. Corporate logos are even found on players' uniforms. But some schools have moved beyond corporate sponsorship of sports to allowing "corporate partners" to place their names and ads on all kinds of school facilities—libraries, music rooms, cafeterias. Some schools accept money to require students to watch Channel One, a news program that includes advertising. And schools often negotiate exclusive contracts with soft drink or clothing companies.

Prompt: Some people argue that corporate partnerships are a necessity for cash-strapped schools. Others argue that schools should provide an environment free from ads and corporate influence. <u>Using appropriate evidence, write an essay in which you evaluate the pros and cons of corporate sponsorship for schools and indicate why you find one position more persuasive than the other.</u>

Analysis: The first thing you should notice about this prompt stem is the verb "evaluate." The prompt is not interested in having you develop an argument in favor or against corporate sponsorship for schools, rather it requests you to assess the pros and cons of the issue and to explain *why* you found one position more persuasive. You should first determine the side you support; then begin your essay by acknowledging the merits of the other side and its pitfalls. This is known as qualifying a stance—a topic more thoroughly explored in Lesson 13: The Qualified Thesis for Waffle Lovers. Many of the AP Language and Composition prompts encourage you to qualify a position because acknowledging the opposition demonstrates a sophisticated understanding of argument construction.

COLLEGE-PLACEMENT PROMPT FROM A LOCAL JUNIOR COLLEGE (www.santarosa.edu/app/placement)

Prompt: Most people have read a book or seen a play, movie, or television program that affected their feelings or behavior in some important way. <u>Discuss such an experience of your own. Describe the book, play, movie, or television program and explain why you regard its effect on you as important.</u>

Directions: Before you begin writing, consider the topic carefully and plan what you will say. Your essay should be as well organized and as carefully written as you can make it. Be sure to use specific examples to support your ideas.

Analysis: In a "describe" prompt, you will be given one of two options: to describe a time when (to tell a story) or to describe something as indicated in the above prompt. Notice that the directions in the previous prompt remind you to use "specific" examples. Your ability to support your assertions with specific examples is the primary concern of this style of prompt. You needn't worry about the topic being so obscure that you'll be left "exampleless," however. These prompts are constructed around generic topics that do not presuppose knowledge of any sort. It would be unfair, for example, for a writing placement test to ask you to describe a recent discovery in astronomy or to describe a trip to a foreign country because these topics require previous knowledge or experience. So, rest assured that the topics will be deliberately generic and vague, but remember that your responses should be chock full of lush examples.

It may seem obvious, but the more you snoop around on the test websites and peek at the released test questions, the better idea you'll have of what type of essay you'll be expected to write. Pay careful attention to the verbs used in the prompts.

Prompt stem verbs are critical to understanding your purpose as a writer. The following chart tells you how to respond to the most common.

Responding to Common Prompts

If the prompt stem verb is . . .	Your essay should . . .
Agree or disagree	take a stance and write a persuasive essay
Confirm (defend) or challenge	take a stance and write a persuasive essay

Take a position on this question	answer the question and support your response in a persuasive essay
Qualify	acknowledge the opposition but still take a stance and write a persuasive essay
Develop your position on this issue	acknowledge the opposition but still take a stance and write a persuasive essay
Describe (discuss) a	identify and detail an object that supports an assertion
Describe a time when	narrate a detailed story that supports an assertion
Evaluate	weigh the pros and cons or the harms and benefits but ultimately conclude by determining to what degree the subject is good or beneficial

What do you have to do?

Practice generating prompts for the SAT, ACT, AP, and college placement exams or just the one that applies to your upcoming on demand writing challenge.

SAT . . .

1. On a half sheet of paper, copy an aphorism from your aphorism journal, a quotation from something you've read in class, or even from an inspirational poster in a classroom.

2. Choose one of the following sets of directions and copy it below your quotation:

- Plan and write an essay in which you develop your point of view on the above assertion. Support your position with reasons and examples from your reading, studies, experiences, or observations.

- Citing examples from your reading, studies, observations, and experiences, agree or disagree with the ideas expressed in the above quotation.

ACT Writing Exam . . .

1. On a separate piece of paper, describe an issue relevant to high school students (e.g., drivers' licenses, work permits, curfew, etc.).

2. Briefly provide two different perspectives on the issue.

3. Conclude the prompt by asking, "In your opinion, should . . . ?"

4. Include these directions after your question:

> In your essay, take a position on this question. You may write about either one of the two points of view given or you may present a different point of view on this question. Use specific reasons and examples to support your position.

AP Language Comp Exam . . .

1. On a half sheet of paper, copy an aphorism from your aphorism journal, a quotation from something you've read in class, or even from an inspirational poster in a classroom.

2. Copy these directions below your quotation:

> Write a carefully constructed essay in which you use specific evidence to defend, challenge, or qualify the assertion.

College Placement Exam . . .

Many junior colleges and state universities insist that incoming freshmen sit for a placement exam that usually consists of a series of multiple-choice questions on grammar and mechanics and an essay prompt that mirrors that of the SAT or that invites students to write an autobiographical narrative. The subject of the prompt must be nondiscriminatory and cannot presuppose knowledge. For instance, the prompts are not permitted to ask the writer to reveal religious beliefs nor are they to expect test-takers to have knowledge of a particular issue like current gas prices.

1.   Begin by making a list of experiences that most humans encounter. (e.g., making a wish that doesn't come true, encountering a roadblock to success, misunderstanding a friend, worrying unnecessarily, etc.).

2.   Choose one of the experiences and plug it into the formula:

     Describe a time when you_____. Vividly recreate the incident with detailed description and conclude by assessing what you learned from the experience.

     It may seem remedial to generate your own prompts for upcoming exams, but the better you get at distinguishing between the particulars of various prompts, the more likely you are to address all parts of the prompt successfully. Besides, no one ever said that thinking like a teacher is detrimental!

13. The Qualified Thesis for Waffle Lovers: Generating Thesis Statements That Acknowledge an Opposition

Many on demand writing prompts give you the options of confirming, challenging, or qualifying a statement. Often student writers argue that they can't support just one side or the other, and they mistakenly assume that a qualified position will allow them to waffle and to argue both sides of an issue.

Being able to approach an on demand writing prompt as an exercise rather than an expression of your deepest feelings is a good first step to avoid the waffling position. This is not to say, however, that you should completely divorce yourself from any buy-in to the topic. Finding a foothold of an argument on one side of the issue can often lead to strengthening your position on the other side. This is your goal in crafting a qualified thesis.

Why should you care?

Even the lowest passing score on a standardized rubric demands that the writer "upholds a consistent point of view." If you are ambivalent on your position, you are best served by qualifying a claim rather than admitting your uncertainty—which can lead to failure.

What do you have to know?

Acknowledge that a qualified claim *is* a point of view and appreciate how a qualified position gives strength to an argument as well as providing structure. Let's say Peter is arguing with his father about staying out late on Friday night. He could say:

"Dad, I am responsible—I won't do anything stupid."

If he's smart, however, he'll qualify his argument:

"Dad, I know you're worried about me doing something stupid, but you've taught me to be responsible, and I've been waiting for this opportunity to show you."

Peter has not only addressed his Dad's argument about responsibility, but if his Dad is still reluctant to say "yes," Peter has provided a structure for the rest of his argument. He could then provide examples of how he was taught responsibility and follow those with the claim that Friday night would provide an excellent opportunity to prove his responsibility.

If you've ever been accused of waffling or not having a clear position, you know that this can be extremely frustrating, especially if you've spent more than 30 minutes writing an essay. To ensure that wafflers develop a point of view in their essays, I encourage them to "qualify" the claim by writing a qualified thesis. A qualified thesis acknowledges a valid argument on the opposing side, then it asserts the writer's position.

Qualified thesis statements save time and set parameters for the writer of an argument. To illustrate, here is the sample SAT writing prompt from The College Board website:

> Are people motivated to achieve by personal satisfaction rather than by money or fame? Plan and write an essay in which you develop your point of view on this issue. Support your position with reasoning and examples taken from your reading, studies, experience, or observations.

A sample *waffle-lover's* thesis might read:

> Both money and personal satisfaction motivate people; it's hard to say that one is more important than the other.

A sample *qualified t*hesis would read:

> Although money may initially motivate people, tending the fires of personal satisfaction keeps people achieving even when they've earned enough money to survive.

This former waffler now has a position and structure. The writer can first address how people are initially motivated by money, then transition into why fame remains the perpetual generator of achievement.

To arrive at a qualified response, a writer should list the pros and cons of an argument or the harms and benefits, then determine which list is longer and/or stronger. The stronger list becomes your position, and the weaker list becomes your acknowledged opposition.

Consider the following prompt and the ensuing qualified thesis that acknowledges an opposition:

Prompt 1: Extending High School

In your opinion, should high school be extended to five years? Plan and write an essay in which you support your opinion with reasons and examples from your reading, studies, experiences, or observations.

Sample Qualified Thesis: Although extending high school to five years would require an increase in funding and possibly state taxes, it would save us money in the long run by requiring less college remediation and providing a more capable work force.

Notice how the qualified thesis offers a condensed roadmap of the essay's arguments.

Here's a detailed roadmap following the qualified thesis.

Roadmap Following Qualified Thesis

Supporting Reasons—why the thesis is correct:

1. **Supporting reason—acknowledges the opposition:** Extending high school to five years would cost more.
   example(s):

   - More funding would be necessary to support additional teachers and materials.
   - State taxes would probably have to be increased temporarily to generate the necessary revenue.

2. **Supporting reason—addresses the position:** Increasing high school to five years would save the state money on college remediation.
   example(s):

   - Currently, ill-prepared college students tax the system by requiring remedial courses that are taught by overqualified professors and graduate students.
   - If students' college-readiness was addressed in high school, it would cost the state less because high school instructors are paid less than professors.

3. **Supporting reason—addresses the position:** In the long run, the state would save money with a better-prepared work force.
   example(s):

   - Workers who are better educated require less training and can begin making meaningful contributions to society sooner.

   - Workers who are ill-prepared in basic math and communication skills grow frustrated and are more likely to be fired.

   Conclusion—answers the question, "Therefore what?": Spending the extra money now to thoroughly educate high school students will benefit the state financially in the long run and benefit the students for a lifetime.

Remember, a qualified position is still a position—one strengthened by acknowledgment of the opposition. In addition, when you craft a qualified thesis, your essay is virtually outlined for you.

Here are some words and phrases that naturally lead to a qualified statement:

Although . . .

Even though . . .

Despite the fact that . . .

While it may be true that . . .

Some may suggest that . . ., but . . .

In developing the qualified thesis, you should provide a lopsided amount of support in favor of your position. The key to successful qualified positions lies in spending more words and ink on the examples and arguments that support the second half of your statement. Imbalance is the key to avoid waffling.

As illustrated in the following Good, Bad, and Fluffy examples of staking a qualified position, you may find this strategy useful when trying to reason your way out of a double shift at your weekend job. Just remember to keep your arguments in lopsided proportion to your position as indicated in the good sample:

The Good—a healthy imbalance in favor of the position

> Although I'd love to help you out by covering the double shift on Saturday, I've already promised my dad that I'd teach him how to text that afternoon. The poor man can't even find the messaging button on his phone, and it's becoming the only way my little sister will communicate with him—so it's pretty important.

The Bad—an unhealthy imbalance supporting the opposition

> Although I'd love to help you out by covering the double shift on Saturday, I've already promised my dad that I'd teach him how to text that afternoon. I know how short-handed you've been and that it's your thirtieth wedding anniversary. I really wish I could fill in for you.

The Fluffy—a waffling balanced response with no clear position

> I'd love to help you out by covering the double shift on Saturday. I know how short-handed you've been and that it's your thirtieth wedding anniversary. But, I've already promised my dad that I'd teach him how to text Saturday afternoon. The poor man can't even find the messaging button on his phone. I'm really torn. I feel like I'm letting you both down—what do you think?

Your Goal—All kidding aside, the more you practice the structure of a qualified claim, the more natural it will become and the more meaningful your arguments will be. And remember, there's never any harm in dining with your opposition, just be sure to serve your position a larger portion of the arguments.

What do you have to do?

Now, try your hand at generating some qualified responses to the following prompts. Begin by answering the series of questions under each prompt before proceeding to the qualified thesis generator.

Prompt 1: Extending High School

In your opinion, should high school be extended to five years? Plan and write an essay in which you support your opinion with reasons and examples from your reading, studies, experiences, or observations.

Questions

• What would be the benefits of extending high school to five years?

• What would be the harms in extending high school to five years?

• Have you listed more benefits or harms?

Qualified Thesis Generator

If you listed more *harms*, plug into the following qualified thesis generator:

Although extending high school to five years would (list 1 *benefit*)

_____,

it would (list 1–2 *harms*)

_____.

If you listed more *benefits*, plug into the following qualified thesis generator:

Although extending high school to five years would (list 1 *harm*)

_____,

it would (list 1–2 *benefits*)

_____.

14. Focusing a Vague Prompt: Writing Qualified Criterion-based Thesis Statements (yes, that's a mouthful)

All right, so you probably took one look at the title of this chapter and said, "Next!" And you're right, it's a convoluted title; ironically the trick that this chapter teaches helps you streamline and focus your essay to give it clarity.

One afternoon I was helping a friend's son prepare for the writing portion of his MCAT—the graduate exam for med school. Interestingly, the essay prompts have nothing to do with medicine or even science. Instead, they ask writers to take a stance on broad philosophical issues. What I discovered was that the prompts insisted that the writers include a way of measuring how their thesis upheld the topic. Truth be told, I got a little bit too excited about this—it's exactly what a debater has to do to win a round.

In debate, teams usually present a case built around a criterion—a means of measuring the validity of their arguments. For instance, given the prompt, "Is it better to be feared or loved?," one team might select a criterion of justice and argue that being feared is preferable to being loved in matters of justice. They might cite how teachers and courtroom judges will be able to demonstrate a greater sense of fairness if they are feared rather than loved. Using that same criterion of justice, the other side could counter that fear implies mistrust and that the individual who is feared must be acting capriciously, which is a far cry from the evenhanded justice being demonstrated. The argument volley would continue, but what's worth noting is the focus that the criterion of justice has given an otherwise tremendously broad topic.

Why should you care?

Standardized essay prompts are often intentionally vague and value-based rather than policy-based in an attempt to avoid privileging previous knowledge. For instance, it's fair for a standardized test to ask you whether you value wealth over health, but it would be unfair for the test to ask you whether you agree with the latest health care reform policy. A criterion-based position helps you focus your response in an on demand writing situation and avoid the amorphous blob that ensues when a writer tries to cover all possibilities in a short time.

If you're still struggling with qualifying a thesis, you may not be up for the challenge of adding a criterion to the mix, but if you are, you will find that your essays maintain a tighter focus.

What do you have to know?

Vague prompts abound on standardized tests since the test-makers' goal is to provide topics that presuppose no previous knowledge and with which everyone is familiar.

Here's a vague sample essay prompt like the ones I was coaching my friend's son on for the MCAT.

> The personal privacy of citizens should be protected from government intrusion. Write a unified essay in which you perform the following tasks. (Task 1) Explain what you think the above statement means. (Task 2) Describe a specific situation in which government might justifiably intrude upon a citizen's personal privacy. (Task 3) Discuss what you think determines when government has a right to intrude upon citizens' privacy and when it does not have a right to intrude.

Note how the above prompt insists that you commit to a criterion in the end. You may, for instance, suggest that only in cases of national security should an individual's privacy be invaded by the government, or you might conclude that a government has the right to intrude on personal privacy if lives are in danger. The possibilities are many, but the result is the same—a clear, measurable claim.

Before you can use a criterion to help focus a vague prompt, you'll need to get comfortable with the term "criterion." Think, for instance, of your criteria for a good friend. You might suggest that a good friend is a good listener, fun, and trustworthy. These would be your criteria—or plural standards—for a good friend. But if I forced you to select only one essential quality of a good friend and you said "trustworthy," you'd now have a criterion—or a single standard by which to measure a good friend, and your basic thesis might state: a good friend is trustworthy.

To qualify the criterion-based thesis, you must acknowledge an opposing criterion. Therefore, a qualified criterion-based thesis about a good friend might sound like this: Although many friends are good listeners, a truly good friend is trustworthy above all else.

Now, the reader anticipates that you will first discuss how many good friends are good listeners, but that truly good friends are trustworthy. You've not only provided a clear measurement for a good friend, you've also provided yourself and the reader with a roadmap of your essay.

To arrive at a criterion, break down the prompt into manageable increments. For instance, if asked to determine whether A or B is more important, ask yourself the following questions:

1. What are some instances when A is more important?

2. What are some instances when B is more important?

3. How can I measure whether the examples under A or B are more important? Some generic questions (which can be used as your criterion) include:

    - Which benefits the most people?

    - Which is most efficient?

    - Which is the most pragmatic?

    - Which has greater lasting impact?

    - Which is most cost effective?

    - Which is the most profitable?

    - Which allows for greater progress?

Let's illustrate the template in response to the following prompt:

Is (A) customer service or (B) quality merchandise more important to a business?

You would begin by asking yourself what are the benefits of each:

1. What are the benefits of customer service?

    - Happy customers

    - Repeat customers

2. What are the benefits of quality merchandise:

    - Customer satisfaction

    - People will pay more for quality

    - Your brand becomes a trusted name that people seek

Since your list under benefits of quality merchandise appears longer and stronger, you seem to be positioned to defend it over customer service.

You would then ask the third question: How can I measure why quality merchandise is more important than customer service? Since the last two items in your list suggest an increase in sales, your answer would likely be profit.

This analysis of the topic would result in the following qualified, criterion-based thesis: Although high-quality customer service may encourage a few repeat customers, investing in quality merchandise is a better way to ensure customer satisfaction and to increase profits for a business.

What do you have to do?

Now, try your hand at generating some criterion-based qualified responses. Begin by plugging in to the above three-step template for determining whether A or B is of greater importance before generating a qualified criterion-based thesis.

Here are some value-based topics to practice responding to:

- Is (A) trust or (B) kindness more important in a relationship?
- Is (A) peace or (B) progress more important to a nation?
- Is (A) equality or (B) fairness more important in education?

If you successfully craft some criterion-based theses, try maneuvering your way through a roadmap for the thesis illustrated in Lesson 13. The challenge will be making sure you maintain the focus dictated by the criterion.

HINT

One way to ensure that your criterion is noticed and aids in the focusing of your thesis is to echo it throughout the essay. For instance, if your criterion is "trust," repeat the word once or twice per paragraph and resist the urge to whip out your thesaurus and make substitutions. While "confidence" and "reliance" may mean essentially the same thing as "trust," there are slight differences, and you want to be sure that you're consistent and clear about your criterion.

CHAPTER 5
Fleshing Out the Essay

Up until this point you have practiced brainstorming topics, mapping out responses, and even generating carefully crafted thesis statements for on demand writing situations. But when the stopwatch is racing, the majority of your time will actually be spent paragraphing the essay.

What follows is a series of lessons designed to help you flesh out your skeletal outlines to on demand prompts. Since your essays will be read quickly and evaluated holistically—often in seconds—it's important to structure your body paragraphs in ways that make your argument clear and your thesis development undeniable. Therefore, the arrangement of ideas and information in a timed essay's body paragraphs can be as important as the ideas themselves. In addition to being coached on how to develop accessible, muscular body paragraphs, you will be instructed on slimming down your introductions and conclusions, and encouraged to routinely title your essays.

15. Lean Lead-ins: How to Write Scrawny Introductions That Pack a Punch

While plunging into the opening paragraph of an essay with nothing more than a well-crafted thesis statement would not be grounds for failure, most evaluators expect an essay to have some form of introduction.

More than likely, you have been taught to begin an essay with a story or personal anecdote that draws the reader into your topic. Many of the best students—those who have traditionally performed well in English language arts—will write introductory paragraphs that cover nearly three-quarters of a page. Many of these students find themselves only halfway through their first body paragraph at the end of their first practice timed essay. They have a hard time knowing how to begin without a hearty first paragraph.

It is possible, however, to whip out brief but compelling introductory statements that satisfy the expectation for an introduction as well as save time that can be more valuably spent crafting body paragraphs and a meaningful conclusion.

Why should you care?

Essays are expected to have introductions, yet on demand writing situations require that little time and ink be spent on opening paragraphs. While the evaluators still appreciate an engaging opening line, none of the standardized rubrics rewards essays for catchy introductions.

These exercises will wean you from previous coaching that an introduction needs to elaborate on the topic and gradually funnel down to the thesis. Often a single introductory sentence followed by a thesis statement is all you need to enter into a timed essay. Once you practice writing "grab and go" introductions, you'll come to rely on their efficiency.

Knowing that several instant introduction generators are available should also lessen the frustration of starting a timed essay.

What do you have to know?

First, reassure yourself that traditional introductory paragraphs are fine if you are given unlimited time to work on an essay, but, with a timed essay, you need new strategies for essay introductions.

The average 30-minute essay consumes about a page and a half of writing. Two–three sentences (including your thesis) tops should be plenty of ink to satisfy your need to introduce your position to your reader.

The following strategies should help you generate an engaging first sentence that, when coupled with your thesis statement (preferably a qualified one!), will result in an efficient yet effective introductory paragraph.

- **Rhetorical question:** Craft a meaningful rhetorical question that strives to focus your argument. If, for instance, your topic was schools should not begin before 9:00 a.m., a meaningful rhetorical question that helps to focus your argument on the academic benefits of a later start time might be: What if the simple addition of one number helped thousands of children learn to add? It's fairly easy to fashion a rhetorical question, so you may be tempted to routinely use one as an introductory sentence. *Be warned*, however. You may actually be weakening the impact of your essay if you're not careful to *avoid* these three common rhetorical question blunders:

  1. Opening with a rhetorical question that rephrases the prompt or asks for the reader's opinion. (e.g., Do you think the school day should start later?)

  2. Overusing rhetorical questions throughout the essay. Rhetorical questions remain an effective strategy if used sparingly; if overused, they smack of uncertainty and weak critical thinking.

  3. Ending an essay with a rhetorical question. The final paragraph of an essay should draw a conclusion from your arguments and examples, not defer to the reader for an opinion (e.g., What do you think the best time to start school would be?)

- **Dinner with the opposition:** Acknowledge a common opposing argument that your thesis will later dismiss. This will also serve to highlight your argument as the more unique position.

- **Sensational detail:** If you have a knack for creative description, offer a detailed description of a scenario in support of your position. The goal is to describe a scene in a single sentence, so curtail the desire to narrate a story and strive to capture a single moment.

- **Startling fact:** If you happen to know a fun fact about your topic, infuse it at the beginning as a way of establishing your credibility on the issue.

- **Quotation:** This is where maintaining an aphorism journal pays off. Recounting a line of poetry, or a song lyric, or an inspirational motto as a point of entry into your topic will not only afford your essay a bit of creative flare, but (depending on the origin of your quotation) also establish you as a well-read, culturally aware writer.

- **Analogy:** Drawing parallels between your topic and something familiar will not only give a creative, memorable opening to your essay, it will also provide you with an example that you can reference throughout your essay and can even serve as a reference point in your conclusion. If your writing has ever been accused of being unfocused, using an opening analogy may be a strategy that helps you maintain focus and develop a logical argument.

- **Literary Allusion:** Referencing a character or scene from literature you've recently studied will offer you a vivid opening illustration and, like the analogy strategy, afford you an example that can be repeatedly referenced throughout your essay.

Read over the following sample introductions that demonstrate how to "skimpify" your opening paragraphs by employing the strategies above. The samples all consist of no more than two sentences, with the exception of the analogy. You'll find that analogies take an additional sentence to make the link between your illustration and your thesis. Be mindful of this link in all of your introductions—even those limited to two sentences shouldn't give the reader whiplash as she segues from your opening line to your thesis. The introductions that follow were created using the following sample prompt and qualified thesis statement:

Prompt: School should not begin before 9:00 a.m. for all public high schools. Plan and write an essay in which you confirm, challenge, or qualify the above assertion. Support your position with reasons and examples from your reading, studies, experiences, or observations.

Qualified thesis: Although a later school start time would also mean a later dismissal, the time spent in class would be more educationally valuable if classes didn't begin until 9:00 a.m.

Skimpified Opening Paragraphs

THE RHETORICAL QUESTION: ASKING A QUESTION THAT LEADS TO YOUR POSITION

If most businesses expect their employees to report for work by 9:00 a.m., why do we expect teenagers to be in their desks ready to work as early as 7:45 a.m.? Although a later school start time would also mean a later dismissal, the time spent in class would be more educationally valuable if classes didn't begin until 9:00 a.m.

DINE WITH THE OPPOSITION: ACKNOWLEDGE AND REFUTE AN OPPOSING ARGUMENT

Nobody will be thrilled to have the school bell ring later for dismissal in the afternoon, but everyone will be glad when the alarm doesn't ring before dawn to begin another school day. Although a later school start time would also mean a later dismissal, the time spent in class would be more educationally valuable if classes didn't begin until 9:00 a.m.

THE SENSATIONAL DETAIL: SHOCK YOUR READER INTO PAYING ATTENTION

The students who nod off during early-morning classes are most likely not dreaming of their lessons. Although a later school start time would also mean a later dismissal, the time spent in class would be more educationally valuable if classes didn't begin until 9:00 a.m.

STARTLING FACT: IF YOU KNOW A BIT OF TRIVIA OR READ A RECENT FACT ABOUT YOUR TOPIC, FLAUNT IT!

Studies show that one of three American teens doesn't get enough sleep. Although a later school start time would also mean a later dismissal, the time spent in class would be more educationally valuable if classes didn't begin until 9:00 a.m.

THE QUOTATION: USE SOMEONE ELSE'S WORDS TO LAUNCH YOUR POSITION

"The early bird gets the worm," but I doubt he could get calculus at 7:45 a.m. Although a later school start time would also mean a later dismissal, the time spent in class would be more educationally valuable if classes didn't begin until 9:00 a.m.

THE ANALOGY: COMPARE YOUR TOPIC WITH SOMETHING ELSE

You don't schedule classes at 7:45 a.m. for the same reason that you don't schedule open-heart surgeries for 11 p.m. If you're after optimum results, students, like surgeons, need to be well rested. Although a later school start time would also mean a later dismissal, the time spent in class would be more educationally valuable if classes didn't begin until 9:00 a.m.

THE LITERARY ALLUSION: REFERENCE LITERATURE YOU'VE STUDIED

Throughout literature, toiling in the wee hours is reserved for deviants like Dr. Frankenstein and Macbeth. Although a later school start time would also mean a later dismissal, the time spent in class would be more educationally valuable if classes didn't begin until 9:00 a.m.

What do you have to do?

Scratch out a qualified thesis in response to the following prompt.

Students' cell phones should be rendered inoperable during school hours. Plan and write an essay in which you confirm, challenge, or qualify the above assertion. Support your position with reasons and examples from your reading, studies, experiences, or observations.

Then develop an opening sentence using the introduction strategies discussed above (remember the analogy may be more than just one sentence in order to connect to your thesis):

- Rhetorical question

- Dinner with the opposition

- Sensational detail

- Startling fact

- Quotation

- Analogy

- Literary allusion

Note which types of introductions are the easiest for you to craft—feel free to skip any patterns that make you struggle. Your goal is to find a few introductory strategies that suit your style and to plug into one of these in your next on demand writing situation.

16. Body Paragraphs That Don't Stand Alone: How to Craft Body Paragraphs That Develop a Thesis

Remember, when you are writing on demand in the shadow of a stopwatch, your readers are scoring the essays under similar time constraints. When body paragraphs in a timed essay begin with claims that reconnect to the thesis, even a rapid-fire reader will be able to notice the supporting arguments clearly.

Ending body paragraphs with an answer to the question "Therefore what?" assures internal conclusions—which can be very helpful if time robs you of composing a thorough concluding paragraph. Responding to the question "Therefore what?" will also force you to reconnect to your thesis, thus ensuring focus.

Framing a body paragraph with a claim and an internally drawn conclusion develops the thesis—provided, of course, that the middle of the paragraph is chock-full of specific supporting detail and meaningful commentary.

Why should you care?

Beginning body paragraphs with claims rather than facts or observations ensures that the thesis is being supported and developed by arguments. Ending body paragraphs with internally drawn conclusions also ensures thesis development and indicates critical thinking—two basic expectations of any standardized rubric.

These exercises in body paragraph structure will give you a framework that is easy to plug into but also meaningful. It may be formulaic, but it's a formula that leads to logical development of an argument or idea.

What do you have to know?

In much the same way that you considered your reader in crafting efficient introductions that served to ease him into your essay, it's imperative that you consider your reader as you address formatting your body paragraphs. The reader is assessing your body paragraphs based on several criteria: thesis development, logic, specific supporting detail, and organization. It's important that you provide the reader with clear evidence of all these elements of a high-scoring essay.

A good body paragraph that develops a thesis begins with a claim. You may remember from Lesson 10 that a claim is an argument, distinguishable from fact or observation, which can't be argued.

HINT

In helping my students distinguish between a claim and an observation, I ask them to imagine two cantankerous old men sitting on a front porch. If one states a claim, the other will surely counter:

"I think it's going to be a dry winter."
"Nope. By the looks of those clouds, storm's a-brewin'."
"Those aren't rain clouds."

Presumably this argument could last all afternoon. However, if one man states an observation, all the other can do is agree and the conversation ends.

"It's raining."
"Yep. Yep, it sure is."

Your goal is to keep the argument alive. Claims, not observations, help you achieve this.

To assist in distinguishing claims from observations, try identifying whether the following statements are claims or observations. To correctly identify a claim, you should be able to answer "yes" when asked: Is this a debatable statement?

Laying Claim to Your Topic Sentences

Instructions:

Place a **C** in the space below if the statement is a **claim**—an assertion that can be disputed (e.g., Writing timed essays is fun!)

Place an **O** if the statement is an **observation**—a fact or statement that can't be argued (e.g., We write timed essays in our English class.).

_____ 1. Writing timed essays prepares us for college.

_____ 2. My cousin Peter had to write timed essays in all of his college classes.

_____ 3. Writing well under time constraints has benefits that extend beyond college.

_____ 4. Timed essays do not necessarily have five paragraphs.

_____ 5. What matters most in a timed essay are specific supporting details.

_____ 6. The more timed essays you write, the more fun they become!

For answers see p. 199

While the first sentence of your body paragraphs is important, remember that the reader is assessing your body paragraphs based on several criteria: thesis development, logic, specific supporting detail, and organization. Ending the body paragraph with an internally drawn conclusion that answers the question "Therefore what?" is a hallmark of keen critical thinking and supports thesis development.

To ensure that your body paragraphs develop your thesis in meaningful ways, consider employing the following formulaic framework:

Body Paragraph Template

CLAIM:

[Is this a debatable statement? _____ If so, how so? . . .]

AT LEAST TWO SENTENCES OF SUPPORT FOR THE CLAIM:

INTERNAL CONCLUSION THAT ANSWERS THE QUESTION: THEREFORE WHAT?

This formula provides the basic structure needed to construct a hearty body paragraph that logically develops a thesis. In the following Good/ Bad/ Fluffy samples that follow, see how a solid claim provides a strong, assertive topic sentence for a sturdy body paragraph, whereas mere observations provide little framework for an argument.

The Good

Strategies for successful on demand writing will continue to be in demand throughout college. College courses, ranging from anthropology to physical education, expect students to be able to write full-length essays in response to test questions. Even if an anthropology course happens to rely on multiple choice testing, there's a very good chance the course will also require a paper or two that—given a college student's cramped schedule—doesn't allow for multiple drafts and will probably be written in a single sitting in front of a computer that one's roommate is impatiently waiting to use to update his Facebook status. Adopting strategies for coping with the demands of timed writing will pay off indefinitely.

> Great paragraph! You begin with a debatable claim and conclude with a statement drawn from the examples and analysis provided in the middle of the paragraph. Your last sentence is not merely a restatement of the topic sentence—it answers the question: "Therefore what?" and provides the reader with what is known as an internal conclusion—my!

The Bad

Many college courses expect students to write on demand. College courses, ranging from anthropology to physical education, expect students to be able to write full-length essays in response to test questions. Even if an anthropology course happens to rely on multiple choice testing, there's a very good chance the course will also require a paper or two that—given a college student's cramped schedule—doesn't allow for multiple drafts and will probably be written in a single sitting in front of a computer that one's roommate is impatiently waiting to use to update his Facebook status. Don't be surprised if a college course expects you to write on demand.

> Uh-oh, your paragraph begins with an observation and concludes with a statement echoing this observation. Notice how your last sentence is merely a restatement of your topic sentence (only with a shift to the informal "you" point of view)—it provides no conclusion, no argument development, and no reason to consider it part of a passing essay. Ouch!

The Fluffy

Successful on demand writing skills will come in handy in timed essay situations in college. College courses, ranging from anthropology to physical education, expect students to be able to write full-length essays in response to test questions. Even if an anthropology course happens to rely on multiple choice testing, there's a very good chance the course will also require a paper or two that—given a college student's cramped schedule—doesn't allow for multiple drafts and will probably be written in a single sitting in front of a computer that one's roommate is impatiently waiting to use to update his Facebook status. Students will be glad they have timed essay writing skills in college.

Your first sentence attempts to make a claim, but the notion that timed writing skills will come in handy in timed writing situations is not really disputable, therefore it lacks the assertive quality of a good topic sentence. The last sentence of the paragraph also fails to draw a conclusion, leaving the reader to draw her own. Strive to answer the question: "Therefore what?" to generate a conclusion to your paragraph

Using the above template, here are two consecutive body paragraphs from an essay advocating the following thesis:

Although a later school start time would also mean a later dismissal, the time spent in class would be more educationally valuable if classes didn't begin until 9:00 a.m.

Sample Good Body Paragraphs That Develop a Thesis

BODY PARAGRAPH ONE

Claim: The benefits of starting the school day later outweigh any harms of ending the day later. **[Is this a debatable statement?** *Yes. One could argue that the harms outweigh the benefits.***]** Although, ending the school day later may be problematic for older students who work or for athletes who may have to miss part of their last class of the day, this would only affect a small number of students. Whereas a later start time benefits all the students with much needed rest—and even the teachers who may have been up late the night before chaperoning that basketball game. **[Therefore what?]**

Internal Conclusion: The inconvenience to and impact on a few students who bag groceries or play badminton are minor compared with the healthy effect of a full night's rest on a brain expected to both be awake and to perform at its best. *[Notice how the internal conclusion doesn't necessarily have the word "therefore" in it.]*

BODY PARAGRAPH TWO

Claim: Students and teachers who have had the recommended 8–9 hours of sleep perform better than those who are sleep-deprived and relying on caffeine to keep their chins from hitting their chests. **[Is this a debatable statement?** *Yes. One could argue that currently students and teachers manage to stay awake and perform.***]** Studies have shown that the teenage brain is hardwired to stay awake late at night and to come to consciousness after sunrise. Just because students must wake early doesn't mean they were able to go to bed early, resulting in sleep-deprived brains that function below capacity in academically demanding classes like trigonometry or biology.

Internal Conclusion: that could make or break a student's future. **[Therefore what?]** Extra sleep translates into extra learning.

What do you have to do?

Use this qualified thesis as a starter for a body paragraph that follows the paragraph template above:

> While the bulk of essay writing currently happens in high school literature classes, essay writing skills should be reinforced across the curriculum to better prepare students for college.

If you'd rather start from scratch, select a prompt from Appendix 1, carve out a qualified thesis, then follow the paragraph template to write a supporting body paragraph.

17. So What?: How to Write Meaningful Conclusions

Odds are that you've been coached on how to end essays. Odds are also pretty good that those methods won't work for on demand writing.

Two of the most common conclusion strategies are highly ineffective for timed essays. The first is to summarize previous points, or "tell 'em what you told 'em." Not only does this strategy fail to draw a conclusion, it is unnecessary in such a brief essay. In a timed essay, the writer is lucky to have made two or three claims; an adept evaluator doesn't need a review of these points when she can simply glance at the page and see them for herself. A 10-page term paper may benefit from a summary of the major ideas; a three-to-four paragraph essay does not.

The second strategy commonly taught to students who have been coached on the five-paragraph essay structure (introduction, three supporting body paragraphs, conclusion) is to reiterate the thesis statement. However, beginning and ending with the same statement creates a circle, not an essay. Circular reasoning is a serious logical error and definitely will not improve your critical thinking score on the rubric.

In fairness to the teachers who have done a fantastic job of preparing you for the rigors of writing in high school, I do not wish to debunk their instruction on how to conclude an essay. However, I do want to urge you to adopt a new strategy for concluding a piece of timed writing. I call this the "So what?" strategy.

I've also seen kids' scores skyrocket on various tests when the only change they've made strategically is to retool their approach to conclusions. When you conclude by addressing the question "What should we do or think?"—you've given the reader a reason for having endured your essay. You've added meaning to your argument. And, you've probably improved your score!

Why should you care?

A meaningful conclusion is an essential part of an essay. An essay that trails off or simply circles back to the original thesis demonstrates a lack of critical thinking and may seem unfinished—because it is! Since one of the goals of an on demand writing task is to measure whether the student can thoroughly answer a prompt in the allotted time, a solid conclusion may be your best shot at proving this beyond a doubt.

The last element an evaluator reads before scoring an essay is the conclusion. It stands to reason that those final words should be meaningful and cogent, not merely a rehash. Rehearsing a few simple questions that can be asked and answered—literally in a matter of seconds—is worth the time and trouble if it means compelling the reader to consider the impact of the points discussed throughout the essay.

What do you have to do?

As you read newspaper editorials or sports columns, notice that these relatively short pieces of persuasion do not summarize their points or repeat their original thesis in the concluding paragraphs. The writers will sometimes advocate a change in policy, call the readers to action, or make a projection for the future. While their strategies vary, they never merely summarize or repeat their initial thesis.

To ensure that your conclusions do more than summarize or repeat previous information, be prepared to give the reader a reason for why he is reading your paper. You can do so by answering one of the following questions:

- So what? Now that several arguments have been proved, what conclusion should the reader draw?

- Now what should we do?

- Now what should we think?

- If you do not agree with my position, then what will happen?

Regardless of which question you chose to answer, you should take comfort in the fact that you will be exiting your essay with a meaningful extension of your argument. This is not to suggest that you've introduced a new argument in your final paragraph—a taboo in any writing circumstance. You are simply drawing your answer to the question from the information previously provided in the body of your essay.

To illustrate how many different options are available for drawing a meaningful conclusion to an essay, the following sample conclusions were derived from the same thesis.

Sample Conclusions

SAMPLE THESIS:

Although starting school later means that the dismissal bell would ring later in the afternoon, the time spent in class would be more educationally valuable if classes didn't begin until 9:00 a.m.

SAMPLE CONCLUSIONS:

SO WHAT? — WHAT CONCLUSION SHOULD THE READER DRAW?

Starting school later in the morning could be just the boost that many students need to get more out of their high school experience. This boost is guaranteed to be stronger, longer lasting, and more beneficial to students than the temporary kick of the triple espresso they guzzle to stay awake during first-period government.

NOW WHAT SHOULD WE DO?

If given the chance to vote for a change in the school start time, vote in favor of helping students learn more—vote yes.

NOW WHAT SHOULD WE THINK?

Sleep deprivation is a serious condition that impairs learning. If we think starting school at 9:00 a.m. will only indulge already lazy teenagers—we must think again.

IF YOU DO NOT AGREE WITH MY POSITION, WHAT WILL HAPPEN?

(Failure to agree with my position may result in . . .)

If we ignore the research that advocates a later school start time, if we ignore the students who awaken in a puddle of their own drool when the second-period bell rings, then we are ignoring the educational future of our children.

Consider making it a habit to answer "What should we do or think?" at the end of all of your persuasive writing. It not only logically culminates your thesis, it rewards readers with a reason for reading your paper.

HINT

Old habits are sometimes hard to break. If you have
trouble resisting the urge to restate your thesis or to
summarize your points, it's not the end of the world
as long as you follow up with a meaningful conclusion
by answering one of the above questions. At all costs,
however, avoid the cop out conclusion: "You decide."
For me it's the equivalent of ending a spellbinding
story with the words, "and it was all a dream."

What do you have to do?

Read the sample student essays in Appendixes 2 or 5. You'll notice the high-scoring
essays already have meaningful conclusions. Take one of the low-scoring essays
and replace the concluding paragraph with one that answers one of the following questions:

- So what?—what conclusion should the reader draw?

- Now what should we do?

- Now what should we think?

- If you do not agree with my position, what will happen?

18. Taking Time to Title: How Titles Provide Focus to an Essay

Would you have bought this book if it didn't have a title? Unlikely. It's also unlikely that you would read newspaper articles, magazine stories, or even novels if they didn't have titles. So why should we ignore titling when writing on demand essays?

Titles show ownership; they give the essay a finished quality. If crafted well, a title can allude to the topic of the essay while enticing the reader. If included in a timed essay, a title conveys both completion and the added bit of focus needed to satisfy the evaluators.

Why should you care?

Extracting a phrase or a few words from the end of an essay and slapping them at the top of an essay takes seconds. If this simple action can guarantee a sense of careful crafting for a timed essay, add focus to the piece, and possibly intrigue or entice the evaluator, these are seconds well-spent.

Standardized rubrics used to assess on demand writing reward writers for being focused. When an evaluator reaches the end of an essay and hears an echo of the title, he perceives that the essay was carefully crafted—from beginning to end. Of course, the truth is that it was beautifully crafted from end to beginning.

What do you have to know?

Imagine yourself walking down a hallway in your school. A stack of student essays has been dumped onto the floor (probably by a frustrated English teacher). You lean forward and see the following titles:

"Shakespeare Gets Saucy"
"Honors English Period 3 Essay"
"The King Is the Real Villain"
"Character Analysis of Macbeth"
"Murder and Mayhem"

Which one do you pick up? I think it's obvious that the one entitled "Honors English Period 3 Essay" is not in your hand. Titles entice us to read what follows. In an on demand essay, however, they serve the additional purpose of offering a focus, especially if the title is extracted from something expressed in the conclusion of the essay. A cleverly wrought title tells the reader that the piece of writing that follows is probably well-crafted as well. A title gives the reader an "ah-ha" feeling at the end of an essay when suddenly the meaning of a title becomes clear.

One of the best places to extract a word or phrase for a title is the conclusion of the essay. You may recall from the last chapter that I cautioned you not to end an essay where you began lest you create a circle, not an essay. That still holds true, but rest assured, a title isn't a restatement of your thesis or main points; it's an abstraction or a phrase that may not be made entirely clear until your last paragraph. Aside from the satisfied sense of "ah-ha!" a reader gains by discovering your title in the final paragraph, it makes logistical sense in a timed situation for you to extract a title from the last few lines you've just written because you won't have time to conjure something brand new.

A good title arouses the reader's curiosity and interest. It does more than simply announce the topic or the writer's position on the topic. I must contend, however, that a lackluster title is still preferable to no title at all!

Read the sample conclusions borrowed from the previous chapter and note their corresponding sample titles.

Sample Conclusions and Titles

SAMPLE CONCLUSION #1

Starting school later could be just the boost that many students need to get more out of their high school experience. This boost is guaranteed to be stronger, longer lasting, and more beneficial to students than the temporary kick of the triple espresso they guzzle to stay awake during first-period government.

POSSIBLE TITLES FOR CONCLUSION #1:

The Good "A Beneficial Boost" It borrows two key words from the conclusion and combines them into a catchy alliteration.

The Bad "Starting School Later" It simply repeats the topic without even hinting at the writer's position. Are you in favor or against a later school start time?

The Fluffy "Getting More Out of the High School Experience" This title simply repeats a phrase found in the conclusion, but it still serves to focus the essay.

SAMPLE CONCLUSION #2

Sleep deprivation is a serious condition that impairs learning. If we think that starting school at 9:00 a.m. will only indulge already lazy teenagers—we must think again.

POSSIBLE TITLES DERIVED FROM CONCLUSION #2:

The Good "Will We Be Indulging Lazy Teens?" It arouses the reader's interest by posing a question that you promise to answer.

The Bad "Starting School at 9:00 a.m." This title states the topic and nothing more. The reader is given no indication of whether the 9am start time is good or bad.

The Fluffy "Think Again!" This title will work, but it's fluffy in that it's a trite repetition of the last two words of the essay. If it's all you have time for, however, it's definitely better than nothing!

SAMPLE CONCLUSION #3

If we ignore the research that advocates a later school start time, if we ignore the students who awaken in a puddle of their own drool when the second-period bell rings, then we are ignoring the educational future of our children.

POSSIBLE TITLES DERIVED FROM CONCLUSION #3:

The Good "A Bleak Future" This title alludes to outcome of the essay's conclusion without repeating the last line verbatim.

The Bad "A Puddle of Drool" This title may be amusing, but it may distract the reader to focus on a vivid but otherwise insignificant detail, the puddle of drool.

The Fluffy "Do It for the Children" This title's tired sentiment deems it a cliché.

HINT

When you title an essay, the title receives no additional punctuation. It may contain a comma or maybe even an exclamation mark or question mark just like any other phrase or sentence, but avoid adorning your title in any other way—no quotation marks, no underline, no funky font changes—nothing! I like to remind my students that their titles should be naked.

What do you have to do?

Consult the conclusions you wrote for the previous chapter and craft some titles. Strive to arouse the reader's curiosity and interest as you write titles. Consider whether the titles you have crafted serve to clarify your position rather than distract the reader.

Rifle through your portfolio and re-title any essays that were denied the full impact of a creative title.

Look at the sample student essays in Appendixes 3 and 6 and offer new titles—especially for the low and middle scores.

CHAPTER 6
Sitting on the Other Side of the Desk

The most valuable writing lesson that I learned as a college student came when I signed on for a part-time job as a reader for a local high school district's proficiency exam. The exam consisted of a 45-minute timed essay. I was trained on how to use a rubric and instructed to make no marks on the essays—I was only to use my pen to note scores in a tiny box.

I had been asked to sit on the other side of the desk—the teacher's side. I realized how much overall organization and specific supporting examples mattered and how little a few misspelled words or misplaced commas counted in on demand writing. As someone who routinely agonized over spelling (regularly writing a spelling demon like "occurs" in the margin of my essays two or three times before settling on a version that I still wasn't sure of) on my term papers, I felt freed. Freed of unnecessary (does that word have one or two "c's"?) worry, freed of the notion that every stroke I put on paper was going to be scrutinized as closely as my 12-page research papers, and freed of the misconception that on demand writing was just like every other essay—only it was written faster and prone to more hand cramping.

The goal of this brief section is to invite you to the other side of the desk by first promoting an internalized sense of timing so that you are never surprised by the clock during an on demand writing session, and second, by encouraging you to read and score other students' work to help you gain perspective on what matters and what doesn't when a reader is scoring your essays.

Once you sit on the other side of the desk, you will never want to go back—there's too much agonizing and fretting on that side.

19. To Know the Clock Is to Beat the Clock

I'm willing to bet that you don't keep a stopwatch in your bathroom or even a clock for that matter. Yet, on any given day when you hop into the shower before school, you have an innate sense of how long it's taking you to get ready. You probably know that you can shut the bathroom door and emerge, bathed and blow-dried in 17 minutes. You can probably sense if you need to skip the mouthwash because you spent too much time searching for that bottle of shampoo under the sink.

This lesson will encourage you to develop this same sense of innate time for your on demand writing situations. Pacing yourself through writing an essay is no different than pacing yourself during your morning routine. But, like your morning routine, allowing yourself to get snagged on a single step can detract from your overall success. If you're rushing to meet your carpool, it's not the day to experiment with a new leave-in conditioner; similarly in an on demand writing situation, you don't want to pause to cross out a paragraph and begin again.

Several years ago, I realized that my debaters and extemporaneous speakers worked better under time constraints than my writing students because they had an internalized sense of time developed by coping with distractions.

In a debate round, debaters are given a limited amount of prep time—often in 30-second intervals. This time allotment is called out by a judge or timer in the room (e.g., "sixty seconds of prep time remaining"). While debaters speak, the judge often slaps the desk or holds up fingers to announce how much time has elapsed. At first, all this commotion is terribly annoying. However, after a few rounds, the debaters develop an innate sense of what a six-minute speech or a three-minute rebuttal "feels" like. They'll come back from rounds and tell me that they know the timer flubbed up and was off by a minute or 30 seconds. Those seemingly distracting time signals and annoying interventions actually let them develop an internal pace-setter that helps them manage their speech and preparation time more efficiently and with less anxiety. Although you may characterize this initial time sensitivity as annoying, in the end it will pay off as you develop an innate sense of pacing needed to succeed in an on demand writing situation.

Why should you care?

Even the most creative and competent writer can be stymied by a test proctor's announcement of: "Two minutes remaining." Being conscious of the time allows you to be in control of the time. Coaching yourself to internalize the intervals of on demand writing will allow you to confidently stride to the next step of an essay rather than stumble into a final paragraph that may decide your future. You will be able to sense when mapping time is over and when the paragraphing must give way to those last two minutes of proofreading.

What do you have to know?

With only 25–40 minutes to craft an essay, you need to allocate your precious time, but before you can do so, you must be able to pace yourself. Pacing oneself comes from being able to sense how much time has elapsed. Unfortunately, the only way to build this awareness is to interrupt your writing process with a noisy or large intrusive timer or stopwatch. (Your cell phone probably comes equipped with a stopwatch feature or log onto http://www.online-stopwatch.com/full-screen-stop-watch for a large flashy digital stopwatch.) What is important is that you become conscious of the stopwatch. Don't be surprised if this stymies your writing at first; it can be frustrating to see how quickly the seconds are flying by. But remember, this is just training you to internalize time intervals—writing the perfect essays can come later.

Try conditioning your writing with the following regime (this procedure was designed for practicing with the SAT 25-minute essay). You can modify it for the timed essay of your choice.

1. Set your stopwatch to beep after 20 minutes (5 minutes before the official end time).

2. Start your stopwatch and take 5 minutes to break down the prompt and road-map your response on a piece of scratch paper.

3. After 5 minutes, begin paragraphing the essay.

4. After a total of 20 minutes have elapsed, let the beeping of the stopwatch interrupt you; realize you now have 5 more minutes to finish. If you haven't started the concluding paragraph, do so.

5. In the final 2 minutes, title the essay and proofread if you can.

What do you have to do?

Try practicing beating the clock with existing homework. It doesn't matter if it's trig or world history—whatever your favorite subject, settle yourself at your desk with your homework and set a stopwatch for half the amount of time you think it will take to complete the assignment. If you begin by underestimating the time actually needed, you'll be guaranteed to feel rushed; with the odds stacked against you, the competition is a true challenge between yourself and the stopwatch. If you have 20 trig problems that you anticipate taking 30 minutes to finish—set your timer for 15 minutes. Then try to beat the clock. During this time, do not allow yourself to be interrupted. Resist the urge to answer your phone, reply to a Facebook post, or exit the building because the smoke alarms are blaring. Stay anchored in your chair, fingers cramped around your pencil, eyes focused on the paper except to occasionally glance at the countdown on the stopwatch.

These frantic sessions should be repeated frequently. Soon you'll begin to have some success in beating the clock—what's more, you'll be getting your homework done faster.

HINT

If your teachers permit it, ask if you can have a stopwatch running during your next timed essay. If this means asking to have your cell phone on your desk during a test, don't be surprised if a teacher says no. A simple digital wristwatch or a kitchen timer will work as well and not arouse your teacher's suspicion that you're cheating.

20. Students as Peer Coaches: Scoring Other Students' Essays

You've more than likely been asked to peer edit another student's essay in your language arts class. Within seconds, you probably noticed if the essay you were reading was better or worse than the one you wrote. Although not asked or expected to do so—you were evaluating that peer essay—you were noticing what to add or avoid in your own essay.

Sitting in the evaluator's chair will give you a different perspective for on demand writing. You will begin to see that handwriting and clear organization count for more than a precisely chosen word or remembering how to use a semicolon.

Why should you care?

Two things happen after students score each other's essays. They begin to see what it takes to get a higher score, and they gain confidence in their ability to know what a high score looks like. Being able to self-assess your work should be your ultimate goal.

What do you have to know?

Whether you ever lift a pen to actually score an essay, you should read and scrutinize the scoring rubric for the test you plan to take or the essay you have to write. In considering both the SAT scoring guide (Appendix 2) and the ACT scoring rubric (Appendix 5), you'll notice that each has a clear break between a passing score and a failing score. While a 4 is considered adequate and passing, a 3 is not.

The first step in understanding a scoring rubric is to determine what distinguishes between a 3 and a 4. Lack of supporting examples, poor organization, and failure to maintain a clear position are all reasons that an otherwise hearty and seemingly technically accurate essay may receive a 3 rather than a 4. Take the time to read over the scored essays in the appendix or online at the College Board website to strengthen your sense of what constitutes a passing essay. Pay particular attention to what surprises you about the passing or failing essays. If you find yourself thinking, "Wow, I would've failed that essay with a 2, but the College Board gave it a 4," investigate why. The scores in the back of this book as well as those on the testing services' websites are annotated with the reader's justifications for the scores. Read these explanations. You will be able to better understand what you should be worrying about and what you can relax about in your next timed essay.

The second step to understanding a scoring rubric involves careful study of the reasons and reasoning for awarding the highest score. What makes the difference between a 5 and a 6? Both are high scores, but if you're reaching for the top of the rubric, what must your essay include? Sophisticated critical thinking (demonstrated by acknowledging opposition), precision in word choice, and varied sentence structure are the key components of the highest scores.

If you do plan to read and score essays—even those in the back of this book—put your pen down. Read the essay briskly and holistically like a professional reader employed by the testing service. Before you determine the essay's score, remember that the readers are told to "reward the writer for what he or she has done well." Be wary of being hypercritical—instead, concentrate on how the essay compares with the high, middle, and low papers you've already studied.

What do you have to do?

In a perfect world, you and a group of similarly dedicated students would gather on the weekend to write essays, swap, and score them. Of course, if this not possible or if such activity would be a death warrant for your cool factor, you can score the student essays that I've reprinted in the appendixes. Appendix 2 offers you three essays in response to an SAT style prompt; Appendix 6 offers three in response to an ACT style prompt.

Before you read the student essays, review the following procedural steps for scoring an essay:

1. Familiarize yourself with the specific rubric.

2. Make notes on the language of the rubric that help you distinguish a 4 from a 5 and a 3 from a 4. For instance, on the SAT rubric, a 4 essay includes adequate examples, while a 3 does not.

3. Resist the urge to peek at the final scores (found in Appendixes 3 and 6) for the essays until *after* you've scored them.

4. Read through each essay briskly; do not pause to take notes or to mark on the essay—even if you see an obvious error, and you will!

5. Upon finishing an essay, immediately determine its score based on the appropriate rubric. Jot down the score on a piece of scratch paper and note a few of the reasons why you gave it the score you did. When you turn to the appendix to see if your scores match those of the other evaluators, you will see the scores explained using a T-scoring method.

    A T-score is a brief evaluation of a piece of writing that includes at least one compliment and one suggestion for improvement based on the rubric being used. The suggestion should reference the item on the rubric that kept the paper from achieving the next higher score on the rubric. If you choose to use this method, here's a template:

+	**Score**	−
compliments based on the rubric		suggestions for improvement based on the rubric

6. When you compare your scores with those in the appendix, don't worry if they're not a direct match. However, we should agree on which were the high (6–5), medium (4–3), and low essays (2–1).

7. Take the time to read over the T-scores as well. Although I sanctioned the scores, student editors initially read and T-scored the work. Compare their comments with yours.

21. Self-editing: Taking a Timed Essay to a Final Draft

You may be surprised to find a lesson on editing in a book on timed essay writing. All of the strategies that you have learned for on demand writing are effective for multiple draft papers as well. Crunched for time, you may find yourself whipping out a first draft in 25–30 minutes, then striving to polish it for a final submission to your instructor. Or, your teacher may assign an essay to be written in class—under time constraints—then invite you to take it home for revision.

Either way, it can't hurt to be equipped with some self-editing tools to help you revise papers when your mom's busy or that smart kid who sits next to you in class is absent.

Peer-editing can be very beneficial for both writers and editors; however, many times writers become passively engaged in peer editing groups—pass your paper on to others and count on them to find what's wrong with it and correct it. To wean you from this passivity, you will be encouraged to first reflect on your essays' strengths and weaknesses and to follow a sequence of steps to self-assess and remedy problems to enhance your existing work.

Why should you care?

Weaning yourself from dependency on others—friends and teachers—to tell you what to improve in a final draft is an important step to gaining competency in writing. When you continually self-edit, you'll begin to develop a tendency to edit as you write. This may mean a few more cross-outs and arrows as you adapt to the "editor's voice" inside your head, but, in the end, you'll have achieved greater precision even in timed writing situations.

What do you have to know?

First and foremost, you *must* know how your essay will be assessed. If the teacher has not already given you the grading rubric or grading criteria for a particular assignment, ask how the work will be graded. This is a reasonable request of your instructors, and one they should be equipped to answer.

Second, consider how much weight is given to each element on the teacher's grading rubric. Does an introductory paragraph count as much as a conclusion? Are vocabulary and sentence structure being assessed? In short, you are creating a checklist of what to address in your revision and where you should spend your time.

Once you have established how your teacher will be scoring your essay and which elements are of critical importance for your grade, you should be prepared to take the next step to becoming your own autonomous editor—putting your essay draft through a self-editing process. The Self-editing Guide below will assist you in revising a generic essay. Allow it to serve as a checklist for any essay you're able to take beyond the one-draft stage. Not only will it help you polish your take-home essays, it will help you internalize and reinforce the features of a solid, well-developed essay—the kind you are ultimately striving to create the first time around in an on demand situation.

Self-editing Guide

1. Read your essay *aloud* with a pen in your hand to make corrections. This may sound odd, but it will help you catch awkward-sounding phrases or poor word choice. Reading aloud forces you to slog through your prose at a slower rate, thus you'll also be likely to "hear" where body paragraphs need more analysis or examples.

2. Look for the following:
   - a failure to begin a body paragraph with a claim, ask yourself if the statement is debatable (if not, scrawl a reminder in the margin "debatable!").
   - a missed opportunity for proof or an example (scribble in the margin "ex?" or "more!").

- insufficient analysis or commentary (write these questions in the margin to goad you into deeper thinking: "how so?" "significance?" " why?").

- failure to draw an internal conclusion at the end of body paragraphs or to connect back to the thesis (jot "therefore what?" at the end of the offending paragraphs).

- bumpy transitions—I like to call these whiplash moments (draw small arrows between the offending sentences and command yourself to "connect!" in the margin).

- conclusion that fails to move beyond the thesis (remind yourself to answer "what should we do?" or "what should we think?" by writing these questions next to your conclusion).

- absent or lackluster title (snoop around in the concluding paragraph for a captivating phrase and steal it as a title for your essay).

3. Now that you've dealt with the content and organization of the essay, it's time to consider your stylistic choices.

   - Place [brackets] around all B.O. in the essay. Even if your teacher has not specified that she is including this in the grading rubric, no one rewards wordiness!

   - Create a list of errors that your teacher wants you to proofread for. If no list is available, consult Lesson 26 "Seven Deadly Sins of Style" or generate a "personalized hit list" of errors that are typically circled in red when you receive essays back. Are you a run-on sentence culprit? Do you overuse the word "that" (I do!). Try to limit your list of corrections to your top three errors, so you're not overwhelmed and can focus on a few significant improvements.

Let's look at the sample self-editing of the following student essay entitled "Keep Playing the Game." The writer was responding to an SAT style prompt and aspiring to the 6-point rubric. Initially her essay was scored a 3 and a 4 by peer editors, who cited her good examples and clear position as plusses and instructed her to clearly support her position with reasons to help develop her thesis.

Sample Self-editing

Prompt: "Attention to health is life's greatest hindrance."

—Plato

Do you agree with Plato? Plan and write an essay in which you develop your point of view on this issue. Support your position with reasoning and examples taken from your reading, studies, experience, or observations.

Keep Playing the Game

Life is filled with adventures, unpredictable

surprises, and endless possibilities, all waiting to be made

into memories. Although most would argue that one's

B.O.

[B.O.]   *health is the most important factor of life, [I believe that]*

B.O.

attention to one's health can [only] halt the possibility of

AGR—"your"   one's
doesn't agree w/   *filling* ~~your~~ *cup of life to the very brim.*
"one's"

B.O.   B.O.
Children are [so] fortunate to have [that] a mostly

CS
CS—replace the
comma after   *careless attitude towards their health* / *it lets them*
health w/a   ^
semicolon   ;

explore and really live. When I was a little girl, my friends

and I would stop at nothing to have a great time. We

would risk our health even if it meant getting bruises up

and down our legs, or maybe dealing with poison oak after

an in-depth forest exploration. All we really cared about

was whether or not we were having fun. To this day, I still

have the same view that life is too short to worry about

No comma needed.

what might happen to my health if I take a risk for a new

**Missed Op
for specific
examples . . .
Do tell!**

opportunity. Although at times I would get hurt while out

adventuring, I cannot imagine my life without the thrill of

really living.

Unlike children, elderly folks sometimes pay too

much attention to their health out of fear of getting hurt

or dying. While I understand this fear, I have found that

[B.O.]

the elderly people in my life have B.O. [really] stopped leaving

their homes and creating new experiences. They get too

used to the same old routine of being careful and

cautionary and forget about the wonderful feeling

of trying something new and exciting. My 75 year-old

Grandma has always dreamed of ziplining through a

CS–replace the comma before however w/a semicolon

jungle in Costa Rica. She has the funds to pursue this

CS

endeavor, however, she pays too much attention to her

Therefore what?

health, which hinders her ability to experience life.

Attention to one's health is life's greatest

hindrance. For some, it is easy to be carefree and live in

Pronoun shift! Rework sentence & replace "you" w/ "we"

only the present, for others, it is more difficult. ~~What I~~

We should eat healthy, take our meds, and most

~~suggest is to eat healthy, take~~ your ~~meds, but for the~~

importantly live life to the fullest

~~most part, live~~ your ~~life to the fullest~~ and create as many

new and challenging experiences as possible. As I've always

Why? What are the rewards of this philosophy?

been told, we should never let the fear of striking out keep

us from playing the game.

HINT

To aid you in locating mechanical and stylisitic errors, try the trick of reading your essay backwards. Begin with the last sentence of the essay and read it from end to beginning, checking for the items on the teacher's grading rubric or the errors that haunt your writing. You'll find that this technique forces you to focus on the structure of your sentences rather than their meaning. It's also another effective way to slow down your reading. Most of us read our own writing too fast to catch mistakes because we anticipate what the words will say.

What do you have to do?

Take an essay you've already written and self-edit for practice. If you've been assigned a take-home essay in a class other than English—such as history or science—apply the self-editing guide to your homework, make a few adjustments, and bet good money that your grade will be higher than it would have been had you submitted your first draft. You will appreciate that this guide to self-editing is fairly universal and not unique to essays written in English class. In fact, one of my former students recently e-mailed me a link to the journal *American Anthropologist* that featured a guide for submissions that was virtually identical to my editing guide. I think what excited me the most was the fact that three years after graduating high school and pursuing an anthropology degree, this student still recognized the characteristics of good writing. And, yes, her paper was published in the journal.

Use the self-editing guide on pages 118–19 as a template for your future editing endeavors.

CHAPTER 7
Reaching the Top of the Rubric

The previous chapters have discussed strategies designed to coach you to a passing score on standardized rubrics for on demand writing. However, if merely passing is not your goal, you can be coached into excelling on the same rubric. The upper echelons of most standardized rubrics look for artful syntactical variety, appropriate and varied word choice, and few, if any, mechanical errors. Essentially, the higher scores reflect sophisticated style.

Stylish writing is an acquired skill—some of you may already possess a sophisticated style worthy of a published writer, others of you may only be equipped with the plodding style of writers experienced at filling in the blanks on worksheets.

So how can you be coaxed into improving your style? Making you aware of simple stylistic blunders like shifts in point of view is an easy first step. Beyond that, however, the most frequently recommended remedy for lackluster style is to read more. Even if your busy schedule limits you to reading only class assigned literature, be sure you really read the texts. Ever notice when you read several pages written by a single author how his or her "voice" seems to be stuck in your head? Well, one strategy for improving your style is to capture and imitate that voice. Those of you taking the Spark Notes shortcut to preparing for class, are shortchanging yourself from developing a more varied and sophisticated syntax.

Improving syntactical variety through sentence modeling will allow you to challenge yourself based on your current abilities. Becoming more verb-conscious can elevate your "skillful use of language, using a varied, accurate, and apt vocabulary" (a.k.a. "diction"). Finally, reviewing the mechanical and stylistic errors that grammar-check programs frequently miss will help you develop skills that will, ideally, carry over to your on demand writing experiences.

22. Maintaining a Consistent Point of View: I OK—You Not!

Ever notice that when people are asked their opinion on a controversial issue, they often hedge and shift from "I" statements to vague claims that contain "you"? For instance, a girl longing for a new outfit might state: "I'd like to shop for a new dress this weekend. *You* can't wear the same dress to both *your* junior and senior proms." Or a boss introducing a new employee dress code might claim, "I want to revisit our dress code policy. You lose respect as professionals if *you* are dressed for a day at the beach." These shifts in point of view indicate a reluctance to own the statements and a resistance to being included in the claim. What's more, the replacement of "I" or "we" with "you" dilutes the impact of the statement.

You may have been told by other teachers to never use "I" in an essay. This makes sense if you were asked to write about World War II or Shakespeare's England; however, when a prompt invites you to cite personal examples or observations—as in the case of SAT and ACT prompts—it's giving you permission to use "I" or "we."

In this lesson, you will build awareness of pronoun usage, learn when to use which point of view, and practice converting informal and inappropriate pronouns to effective ones.

Why should you care?

When I was presenting a workshop on timed essays at a California Teachers of English conference, a woman in the audience introduced herself to me as reader for the SAT exams. She said she was glad that I had addressed the importance of avoiding the pronoun "you." She added that, as a reader, she had been instructed to take an essay down a full notch on the 6-point scale for inconsistent point of view. Ouch!

What do you have to know?

Losing a full point on an essay because of pronoun slippage is a serious threat that's easy to avoid by being conscious of pronoun use. If nothing else, avoid the pronoun "you" in responding to prompts that ask for your opinion. As you can see in the sample sentences from student persuasive essays, using the informal pronoun "you" inappropriately points a finger at the reader and accuses her of some injustice:

- If you want to be prom king, you must be respected by all different types of students.
  Reader's thoughts: Wow! I didn't know that 46-year-old teachers could run for Prom King; I'd better order that tux and polish up my dance moves.

- "If you eat dessert every day, you will not be able to fit in your chair."
  Reader's thoughts: Hey! Who told you about my 12-day ice cream binge? For your information, they do make chairs smaller than they used to.

- "If you don't stop polluting, our world will be destroyed."
  Reader's thoughts: Who knew that I had such powers? They say that teachers change the world—I guess they are right. My excessive trips to the library are going to kill us all.

Appreciate how inappropriate the above claims are. Since you can never predict who will be reading your essays, it's best to avoid the pronoun "you" and all associated accusations.

So what can you use? You have the option of employing the first person—"I" or "we." Or, you can use the third person "one" for a more formal tone. Notice the difference in tone in the following samples:

- **The forbidden "you":** "If you want to be prom king, you must be respected by all types of students."
  The informal first person: "If I want to be prom king, I must be respected by all types of students."
  The formal third person: "If one wants to be prom king, one must be respected by all types of students."

- **The forbidden "you":** "If you eat dessert every day, you will not be able to fit in your chair."

The informal first person: "If I eat dessert every day, I will not be able to fit in my chair."

The formal third person: "If one eats dessert every day, one will not be able to fit in one's chair."

- **The forbidden "you":** "If you don't stop polluting, our world will be destroyed."

  The informal first person: "If we don't stop polluting, our world will be destroyed."

  The formal third person: "If people don't stop polluting, the world will be destroyed."

It's up to you and the tone of your essay whether you employ the informal first person or the formal third person; however, if the subject is impersonal—like World War II or photosynthesis—employ the formal pronoun "one." Be certain to never mix and match first or third person—maintaining a "consistent point of view" is a prerequisite for the highest marks on the scoring rubrics.

HINT

If you're a shrewd reader, you're probably asking yourself, "Why is the very book that's telling me to avoid the informal pronoun 'you' using 'you'?!" That's a good question. The pronoun "you" is permissible in the description of a process; however, it's very unlikely that a standardized test or timed essay prompt will ask you to detail a process. If it does, feel free to ignore this chapter.

What do you have to do?

Experiment with different points of view, rewriting each of the following sentences in the informal first person and the formal third person.

- You must be able to organize your thoughts quickly and roadmap a response to the essay prompt.

- If you prepare in advance with a brain purge, you will have plenty of examples for your essay.

- You should try to begin your body paragraphs with claims, not facts or observations.

- At the end of your essay, strive to answer the question, "Now what?" to offer your readers food for thought.

Now, on a separate sheet of paper, rewrite the following paragraph, converting the informal pronoun "you" to the *first person pronoun* "I." Beware: changing pronouns may also require altering verbs.

You are expected to perform on demand constantly. Employers evaluate *your* ability to respond on demand from the moment *you* first meet in the job interview. Sure, *you'll* never know the exact questions that will be put to *you* in an interview, but *you'd* be a fool not to do a little research about the company or think through a reply to the "tell us a little bit about yourself" question. While it's not uncommon for *you* to pre-think before going into a situation where *you* may have to talk on demand, it is uncommon for *you* to prepare for a situation where *you* may have to write on demand on an unknown prompt. However, preparing for an impromptu situation—oral or written—is not only possible, it's imperative.

Now rewrite the same paragraph converting the informal pronoun "I" to the *formal pronoun "one."* Remember, both the informal pronoun "I" and the formal pronoun "one" are correct as long as they are used consistently throughout an essay.

Maintaining a consistent point of view requires that you never mix and match pronouns. Correct the following sentences by rewriting them with a consistent point of view. Answers should vary as illustrated in the sample responses to the example.

Example: Maintaining a consistent point of view in one's essay is essential for our success on the SAT.

Maintaining a consistent point of view in <u>one's</u> essay is essential for <u>one's</u> success on the SAT.

Maintaining a consistent point of view in <u>our</u> essays is essential for <u>our</u> success on the SAT.

1. If you mix and match your pronouns, the reader will be confused about one's perspective.

2. Confusing one's reader is pretty much a guarantee of a low score on your essay.

3. I have found that avoiding the pronoun "you" helps one maintain consistency and lessen confusion.

4. It doesn't matter if we use formal pronouns or informal pronouns; what matters is that one is consistent.

23. Start Your Modeling Career— Improving Sentence Variety

Not many fashion models were born flawless. With a few enhancements and a bit of airbrushing, however, models become images to envy.

Not many of us were born with the ability to craft spectacular sentences or use amazing syntax. Not all of us are willing to spend the hours at the mental gym, reading highbrow authors, and generating sophisticated syntactical patterns. We are, however, capable of diagnosing our flaws and emulating the great writers who strut their sentence structure and make it look effortless.

Complex sentence structure indicates complex thought patterns. Varied sentence structure demonstrates conscious choice in style. Superior writers are in command of their style rather than coming by it accidentally.

In this lesson, you will be encouraged to take note of professional writers and their unique sentence structures as you read. Then, you'll be instructed in how to imitate and adopt some their sentence patterns as you write.

Why should you care?

Achieving upper scores on any of the standardized tests requires being able to "demonstrate syntactical variety." If you are having trouble catapulting your scores past passing into the superior range, you should consider taking sentence modeling seriously.

What do you have to know?

To get you noticing syntax and appreciating complex sentences, begin to extract or highlight sentences from your readings that are "syntactically splendid." The only criterion is no simple subject-verb sentences. It does not matter if you're reading the sports page or an eighteenth century novel, start noticing and marking sentences that impress you because of their unique structure. They may be extremely short; they may be exceptionally long; or they may intrigue because of their unique use of punctuation, like a string of semicolons followed by a comma as in this sentence.

What follows are a few sample sentences extracted from some of my recent reads. I then chose a topic—in this case, my dog—and modeled the professional sentences as best I could. Try doing the same.

Sample Syntactically Splendid Sentences

- The woman emerged, slowly and deliberately, from the black smudge of a car.

    —Don DeLillo, *Cosmopolis*

    The dog emerged, wet and shivering, from the grease stain of a pond.

- His hair was dead and thin, almost feathery on top of his head.

    —Harper Lee, *To Kill A Mockingbird*

    His fur was damp and matted, almost clumped on top of his head.

- Holding firmly to the trunk, I took a step toward him and then my knees bent, and I jounced the limb.

    —John Knolls, *A Separate Peace*

    Biting tightly on the rope, the dog took a step back and then his jaw strained, and he broke the tether.

- Mercifully, Brunette's path took him outside the courtyard of the hospital where he had brief glimpses of sky and blossoming trees; he wished he could somehow store up the beauty of the plump clouds and take it with him.

    —Donna Leon, *Friends in High Places*

    Graciously, the dog's path took him inside the alley of the restaurant where he smelled the odors of hamburger and rotting chicken; he wished he could somehow store up the joy of his saturated senses and take it with him.

What do you have to do?

Now that you've had a chance to see how sentences are modeled, try extracting some of the all-star sentences you've been noticing in print. Strive to adopt one pattern at a time as your new favorite and imitate it whenever you have the chance—in a thank you card to Aunt Edna, in a physics lab write-up, even on your SAT essay. Try this a few times and you'll find that you not only begin to memorize the sentence patterns, but your Aunt Edna and your physics teacher will begin to think of you as much more sophisticated.

If you are struggling to locate sentences worthy of imitation, here are a few extracted from Andrea Lunsford's *Everything's an Argument*.

Sample Syntactically Splendid Sentences

1. Moving from stated reason to claim, we see that the warrant is the assumption that makes the claim seem plausible.

2. Lack of logic produces a chaotic, arbitrary world, like that of the Queen of Hearts in *Alice in Wonderland*.

3. Arguments can't be stamped out like sheet metal panels; they have to be treated like living things—cultivated, encouraged, and refined.

4. Arguments serve too many purposes, too many occasions, and too many audiences to wear one suit of clothes.

5. When it comes to making claims, many writers stumble—facing issues squarely takes thought and guts.

24. Self-diagnosis of Sloppy Syntax: Reworking Original Sentences

In previous chapters you became conscious of your syntax and aware that you have choices in how you lay down words. Being able to self-diagnose one's own lackluster sentence patterns is the next goal in improving your style.

This lesson will ask you to reflect on the work you've already generated in previously written essays and invite you to individualize your instruction. You might be up for the sophisticated challenge of improving the complexity of your sentence structure, or you might simply be converting "to be" verbs to more vivid choices. Either way, you will be making improvements.

Why should you care?

Becoming self-conscious about your use of the word "things" or the overuse of "to be" verbs will turn on that editorial voice in your head as you write an on demand essay. Ideally, you'll start making substitutions and improve the precision of your diction and your mechanical accuracy.

These exercises can be done independent of a teacher or tutor. These diagnostic tools can be packed off to college, where taking an active—rather than passive—role in your own education is not only encouraged, it's demanded.

What do you have to know?

The more familiar you become with your personal writing flaws the better. Once you can create a "personal hit list" of persistent errors and overused phrases or words, you'll be able to focus on meaningful changes.

The place to begin is with some of your graded writing. Make a list of the errors that instructors or peers are continually circling. Are you seeing some proofreading symbols repeatedly? Do you know what they mean? A quick Google search for standard proofreading symbols will aid you in translating your teacher's comments. For instance, are pronouns continually circled and the word "ref" scrawled above them? If so, you have faulty pronoun referencing and would benefit from replacing your pronouns with specific nouns.

If you have a limited knowledge of grammar or terminology, don't despair. Many online writing labs, like the OWL at Purdue University, offer concise examples of both proofreading symbols and the errors that precipitate them.

What do you have to do?

Select a previously written essay, preferably something you've written in class, like a timed essay or an exam. If you want to use one of the practice essays you wrote for an earlier exercise, that's fine.

Block out 10 sentences to examine and number the sentences. On a clean, lined sheet of paper number every fourth line 1 through 10. This will serve as your revision paper where you can rewrite each of the 10 sentences you blocked out in the original document.

Walk yourself through all or some of the following diagnoses, then strive to improve the ailing sentence(s). Don't be dismayed if you have an abundance of one type of stylistic blunder and none of another. Your style is bound to be uniquely yours!

Diagnoses

Diagnose: Circle the first word of any sentence that begins with the same word as another.

Improve: Choose one of the sentences to reorder and rewrite it next to the corresponding number on the clean sheet of paper.

Diagnose: Draw a square around the verbs in each sentence.

Improve: Experiment with moving one verb before its subject. This may require changing the verb's ending. Transcribe the revised sentence on the clean sheet next to its corresponding number.

Diagnose: Look for a weak, lackluster verb.

Improve: Replace it with a vivid verb and transcribe the sentence onto the list.

Diagnose: Find a sentence that ends with a prepositional phrase.

Improve: Move the phrase to the beginning or middle of the sentence and transcribe the sentence on the appropriate line on your paper.

Diagnose: Search for two remaining sentences that can be combined.

Improve: Using a semicolon or a comma and a coordinating conjunction, combine them into a compound or complex sentence, then transcribe the new sentence onto the list.

Now reassemble your 10 sentences into a cohesive unit and bask in your syntactical improvement!

25. Vivifying Verbs: Improving Diction by Carefully Selecting Verbs

In preparing for your standardized exams, you have no doubt jammed and crammed high-powered SAT vocabulary into your brain—but knowing definitions and being able to use words effectively are distinctly different. In this lesson, you will be coached to focus on carefully selecting precise verbs that can also express tone.

Verbs, unlike strings of adjectives, are efficient in conveying vivid images and offering illustration. For instance while you could write: "the boy trembled with fear and trepidation in the corner," saying instead: "the boy cowered in the corner" paints the picture just as vividly but much more efficiently thanks to the vivid verb "cowered." Furthermore, in on demand writing situations, the stopwatch does not allow for long reflection about precisely the right word or scrolling through a thesaurus. You can waste precious time struggling to remember if you've used "trepidation" correctly in a sentence when a fairly simple verb like "cower" will convey your meaning effectively. By and large, verbs are simple, familiar words that, if chosen carefully, can up the ante on your bet of achieving the criteria of "exhibiting skillful use of language" on a scoring rubric.

Why should you care?

On the SAT and the ACT exams, you will be invited to cite examples from your reading. Most student writers will do so by starting with a lackluster verb, stating that a particular author "uses" a theme or idea. This portion of analysis often lacks the vivid writing of the personal anecdotes that populate the rest of the essay. A few carefully selected verbs can make the inclusion of a literary or nonfiction example as compelling as a personal story.

The highest scores on standardized rubrics for both the SAT and the ACT essay tests demand that word choice be "varied and precise." Unless you are prepared to expand beyond basic utilitarian verbs like "uses" or "contains," then your scores will remain stagnant—below the superior distinction.

What do you have to know?

Appreciate what a difference a verb can make by taking note of what happens to a sentence when the lackluster verb "contains" is replaced by vibrant substitutes:

The essay *contains* vivid description.

The essay *sports* vivid description.

The essay *is flush with* vivid description

Vivid description *permeates* the essay.

Vivid description *saturates* the essay.

Vivid Verbs to Replace "Contains"

Encapsulates	Is infused with
Possesses	Is flush with
Permeates	Is imbued with
Saturates	Is inoculated with
Sports	Is steeped in

Continue to discover what a difference a verb can make by noticing the vivid substitutes for the verb "uses" in the following sentence:

The author *uses* color in her novel to show the characters' moods.

The author *infuses* color in her novel to show the characters' moods.

The author *scatters* color throughout her novel to show the characters' moods.

The author *landscapes* her novel with color to show the characters' moods.

The author *adorns* her novel with color to show the characters' moods.

Applaud what can happen if a writer selects verbs that are metaphorically compatible for use in the same sentence. A bland observation—The writer *creates* a scene by *using* dialogue—becomes a vivid bit of analysis as verbs convey a picture of quilting, planting, or cooking:

The writer *quilts* a scene by *stitching* in bits of dialogue.

> The writer *cultivates* a scene by *planting* lines of dialogue.
>
> The writer *concocts* a scene by *folding* in dialogue.

If you're really out to improve your style, experiment with developing metaphors via vivid verbs. The following verbs have been arranged in "metaphoric clusters" to aid you in this endeavor.

Vivid Verbs to Replace "Use" or "Make"
(arranged in metaphoric clusters)

ornament	whip up	reinforce	sprinkle
decorate	concoct	wield	shower
adorn	fold in	bolster	sling
furnish	blend	fortify	splatter
			dab
plant	formulate	call upon	steep
scatter	inoculate	summon	brew
sow	inject	announce	infuse
cultivate			
weave	employ	populate	
quilt	work	impregnate	
stitch		fertilize	
braid			

What do you have to do?

To raise your consciousness of stylistic choices, underline the verbs in one of your compositions or even in a short homework assignment—then replace a lackluster verb or two.

Make it a habit to single out your verbs and make substitutions. Raising your verb consciousness just may raise your essay scores.

26. Seven Deadly Sins of Style: Catching Errors That Impede Readers' Understanding

Whether it's a scoring rubric for an AP English exam or a junior college placement test, the advice given to holistic readers is to consistently reward writers for what they do well and to dock their score for mechanical errors only if those errors accumulate and impede the reader's understanding.

What follows is a list of seven mechanical errors that are guaranteed to impede a reader's understanding. Since grammar check is not available when you are in an on demand writing situation, you need to learn to avoid these errors. What makes these errors even more troublesome is that grammar check will not alert you to these mistakes in any case because grammar check cannot intuit the intent of a writer.

Why should you care?

Errors that impede a reader's understanding of an essay—that is, mistakes that make a reader stop and start throughout the text—are punishable by lowering the essay 1–2 ranks.

An occasional misspelled word is a forgivable sin; failing to underline the title of the novel *Frankenstein* could mean that an entire paragraph or essay is misconstrued as being about the character, not the book. The seven errors listed below demand your attention because they distract the reader's attention.

What do you have to know?

When you compiled your "personal hit list" of errors in Lesson 24, you probably stumbled across at least some of the following errors. These errors are not only pervasive in student on demand writing, they creep into multiple draft papers as well since they usually evade detection by grammar check.

As you inspect this list and compare it with your personal errors, you'll probably be able to whittle down the list to three or four errors that consistently snag your writing. Let this be a list you're committed to searching for and destroying in your writing.

The Seven Deadly Sins of Style

1. FORGETTING COMMAS WITH COORDINATING CONJUNCTIONS.

Hamlet sulks around the castle, and he ignores his family and friends.

Comma needed

Hamlet sulks around the castle and ignores his family and friends.

No comma needed

Grammar check won't catch this common run-on because the computer can't anticipate the function of the conjunction in the sentence: Is the conjunction joining independent clauses (as in the first sentence)? or two nouns (as in the second)? To curtail this error, try reading your essays backward, isolating the words "and," "but," and "so." Then determine whether what lies on either side of the conjunction is an independent clause—if so, place a comma before the conjunction. If not—leave it alone.

2. IMPROPER PUNCTUATION OF TITLES.

Hamlet is bold and provocative.

Underlining <u>Hamlet</u> indicates the subject is the play, not the man.

I did not sing Like a Virgin!

Placing quotations around "Like a Virgin" clarifies that the writer is referencing a song, not a manner of singing.

Grammar check has no way of knowing if a writer is referring to the title of the work or the character; the reader will be equally confused if one says: "Frankenstein is elegant" or "Beowulf is boring."

HINT

You may be confused by the fact that throughout this book and probably in your teachers' handouts, you've seen the titles of works italicized. In handwritten works (or those done on a typewriter), underlining words indicated to typesetters that these words should be italicized. Today, our computer software allows us to italicize the titles of books, plays, and films. For on demand writing situations, however, you must still underline titles—try as you might, you cannot italicize with a pen.

3. MISUSING APOSTROPHES: POSSESSION VS. CONTRACTION

It's hard drive broke!

Translation: It is hard drive broke! This does not make sense!

Its hard drive broke!

Translation: The hard drive is broken! This is sad!

Both "it's" and "its" are viable, correct choices given their placement. Clarification is easier if you first understand that you are accustomed to using apostrophes in contractions and to show possession with nouns. Possessive pronouns, like "his" or "her" never use apostrophes. Therefore, when using "its" to show possession, never use an apostrophe. Reserve the apostrophe usage with it's for the contraction form of "it is."

4. INCONSISTENT VERB TENSE:

Hamlet sulked around his castle, and then he kills a few people.

The verb tense inconsistency confuses the reader. It is particularly bothersome when writing about literature—which most on demand prompts invite writers to do. Literature, like film and other art forms, needs to be written about in the present tense because for someone somewhere the action is happening for the very first time. "Hamlet is a perplexed young man" is still correct even though by now you know that Hamlet is dead as a ducat.

Once again, you cannot rely on grammar check to catch this error in tense, since the computer cannot distinguish between examples gathered from literature and those borrowed from experience.

5. DISAGREEMENT OF PRONOUNS AND ANTECEDENTS

Everyone should improve their proofreading skills.

The subject of this sentence and its pronoun are in disagreement. "Everyone" is singular; the pronoun "their" is plural.

Someone is a stickler for their grammar rules.

The subject of this sentence and its pronoun are in disagreement. "Someone" is singular; the pronoun "their" is plural.

Native English speakers cannot trust their ears when struggling to make their vague subjects (everyone, anyone, someone, everybody, etc.) agree with their pronouns. Attributable in large part to our loss of this rule in speech, many writers will struggle to find agreement. There are, however, two ways to cure this agreement problem:

First, if you use a specific subject, the problem is unlikely to occur. Journalists are instructed to avoid vague subjects in their writing because it leads to the awkward "his or her" construction—which also uses more ink.

Students should improve their proofreading skills.

The subject of this sentence and its pronoun are agreement. "Students" is plural; the pronoun "their" is plural.

Mrs. Prickly is a stickler for her grammar rules.

The subject of this sentence and its pronoun are in agreement. "Mrs. Prickly" is singular and female; the pronoun "her" is singular and female.

Second, if the subject cannot be replaced, then substitute an androgynous name like "Pat" or "Chris" for "anyone," "someone," "everybody," etc. Then your ear should catch the error and allow you to make the proper choice:

Everyone should improve their proofreading skills

Substitute "Chris" for "everyone" and trust your ear to make the pronouns agree: Chris should improve his or her proofreading skills.

Somebody is a stickler for their grammar rules.

Substitute "Pat" for "somebody" and trust your ear to make the pronouns agree: Pat is a stickler for his or her grammar rules.

Finally, strive to keep your subject plural when possible to avoid the cumbersome "his or her" construction.

6. MISSING COMMAS AFTER DEPENDENT CLAUSES

Forgetting to signal the attachment of dependent clause to its independent clause will cause the reader to misread the sentence the first time through, forcing the reader to reread it. This impedes the reader!

As I read *Hamlet* I fell asleep.

This sentence must be reread to capture its intent.

As I read *Hamlet*, I fell asleep.

The dependent clause is attached to the independent clause with a comma.

Remember the following distinction: When a dependent clause appears before an independent clause, attach it to the main clause with a comma. Keep your commas at home when a dependent clause follows an independent clause.

As I read *Hamlet*, I fell asleep.

This sentence is correctly punctuated.

I fell asleep as I read *Hamlet*.

This sentence is correctly punctuated, too!

7. AWKWARD "IS BECAUSE" CONSTRUCTION

Usually indicative of the passive voice as well as an awkwardly constructed sentence, the phrase "is because" is an easy one to eradicate from your essays, especially after you've been introduced to the stench of B.O. in Lesson 8: Eliminating B.O.

The reason I like Hamlet is because he is witty.

awkward!

I like Hamlet because he is witty.

better!

The reason that many writers make these errors is because grammar check won't correct them.

awkward!

Many writers make these errors because grammar check won't correct them.

better!

What do you have to do?

Review a piece of writing—either your own or a partner's—scouring for the Seven Deadly Sins.

As you may have noticed, it may be easier to find fault with others' writing. Read the sample student essays in Appendixes 2 and 5 and detect their deadlies using the following checklist and accompanying proofreading symbols:

The Seven Deadly Sins of Style Checklist

Instructions: Read an essay and place a √ by those items detected in the text. As you encounter a particular error, indicate where in the essay the error occurs by marking it with the proper proofreading symbol found in the Annotation column:

√	"Sin" Annotation	Explanation
	R.O.	Commas with coordinating conjunctions
	<u>*novels/plays*</u> *"poems/essays"*	Proper punctuation of titles
	's	possession vs. contractions (its vs. it's)
	tense	verb tense (consistency/present tense — literature)
	AGR	Pronoun/antecedent agreement
	^	Commas after dependent clauses
	AWK	Awkward "is because" construction

CHAPTER 8
Practice That Can Make You Nearly Perfect

A two-page exercise in thesis construction or a brief lesson in syntax is unlikely to polish your writing abilities to perfection. Practice—and lots of it—is almost certainly a more effective means of ensuring that you keep your prose buffed to a high luster.

The lessons in this chapter are not unique to timed writing situations. They can be used to improve writing whether or not a stopwatch is involved. The aim of these lessons is not to teach you new strategies but to reinforce concepts that can strengthen all of your writing. You can never get enough practice in being specific, infusing facts creatively, countering arguments logically, and reading analytically.

27. Strive to Specify: Converting Vague Phrases into Vivid Examples

The easiest flaw to remedy in an essay is vague or unspecific writing. Many people, however, think they are being specific when they give an example. If they state, for instance, "Math is difficult for many people," they may assume they're being specific. But, once they're shown the sentence "Trig was so hard that my bother Matt nearly dropped out of school," they begin to see the difference.

This lesson invites you to revisit some of your writing and to infuse more specific details—a simple yet important exercise in becoming a more autonomous self-editor.

Being more specific will not only help you make your writing more interesting and memorable, it will also help you avoid basic lapses in logic like begging the question and circular reasoning. When a specific example is offered rather than a vague reference, it's more likely that commentary or explanation will precede or follow. Thus, employing detailed examples results in well-developed essays.

Why should you care?

When an evaluator holistically reads an essay at a brisk pace, specific, vivid examples stand a greater chance of being remembered and credited to your score.

What do you have to know?

When you recall reading a specific essay or story in class, you are more likely to remember the specific concrete details than the carefully crafted last line or even title. For instance, back in Lesson 21, you read a student essay. Can you remember its title? Can you recite the essay's last line? Can you recall what the writer's grandma had always dreamed of doing? While you may have forgotten the essay's title or its last line, I'm pretty confident that you recalled that her grandma wanted to go ziplining in Costa Rica. We don't forget gems like that.

Why do we remember details like that even when there's no quiz planned? The details paint a picture in our mind—I know when I read my student's essay, I pictured my children's grandmother in a tropically floral pantsuit, her purse secured to her shoulder, careening through the treetops. In my mind, the writer got credit for a specific supporting example. However when she stated, " . . . she pays too much attention to her health" I had no image to accompany this statement, and therefore I didn't log it as a specific example when it easily could've been.

Let's take the vague sentence, "She pays too much attention to her health," and convert it into a vivid example:

> My grandma's so busy calculating the grams of fat and sugar in every bite of birthday cake that she rarely enjoys a family party.

I don't know about you, but I'm more inclined to remember that granny was a downer at birthday parties than I am likely to recall the line "she pays too much attention to her health."

Can a specific example get even more specific? Of course, and it should if it can. Let's take the same vague sentence: "She pays too much attention to her health." Here's one attempt at making it more specific:

> My grandma spends more time attending free blood pressure screenings at the local pharmacy than she does walking her dog or working in the garden.

Not bad.

Better:

> My grandma spends more time attending free blood pressure screenings at Wilson's pharmacy than she does walking her dog Tank or planting zinnias.

Now we have a vivid image of grandma parked in front of Wilson's while her dog Tank languishes beside her drooping zinnias. It's a one-of-a-kind image—the kind you get when you strive to specify.

HINT

At the very least, when in doubt, use specific names. Even ordinary names like John or Mary conjure for the reader an image—an image of the John or Mary who populate the reader's life. Instead of writing, "My teacher hates my writing," try, "Mrs. Prickly hates my writing." Odds are the reader will commiserate with you more.

What do you have to do?

Infuse specific details into each of the lackluster sentences in the exercise below. The vague phrases/words that need to be made more vivid have been italicized.

1. Sometimes *my mind wanders* while I'm writing *an essay*.

2. *I am often surprised* when I receive *a bad grade* on *an essay*.

3. Many *students* would rather *argue about their grade* than *work hard*.

4. Many *teachers* seem *to grade papers arbitrarily*.

5. *Grading practices* can vary from *class to class*.

6. Many *teachers* award *extra credit* to compensate *underachieving students*.

7. Some *students work hard* yet still fail to get *a good grade*.

8. Sometimes *students* neglect to check *what the teacher is grading them on*.

9. Often *participation* in *a class* is *worth more* than a student will think.

10. Being clear on the *teacher's expectations* can ensure *success in a class*.

28. Actual Factual: Infusing Facts and Stats in Interesting Ways

My impromptu and extemporaneous speakers on the debate team are not only expected to include specific data in their speeches, they also are expected to do so in artful, memorable ways. Seeing them transfer these techniques to their persuasive writing has prompted me to coach my writing students on how to include data in their writing in ways that will get the facts noticed as well as aid in developing their thesis.

Some on demand writing situations—like AP exams and the International Baccalaureate—give the test-taker a fact-laden piece of material to read and synthesize, with the writer expected to infuse facts or statistics into the response. If you are well-versed in a particular subject area, you may also wish to use some of your specific knowledge in response to a general prompt. For instance, if you have a passion for biology, you may wish to use some of your specific knowledge of the animal kingdom when responding to an aphorism by Stephen Jay Gould that questions the morality of nature.

Including facts and statistics is often necessary in academic writing. When you infuse specific knowledge, however, you want those facts to have impact. Whether it's a test-taking situation or a persuasive essay, an overabundance of facts and statistics can cancel out their significance; similarly, if the facts are simply stated, they risk losing their impact by essay's end.

This lesson will illustrate methods for infusing facts or details into your on demand writing in memorable ways and invite you to practice the strategies that work the best for you.

Why should you care?

Essays that are holistically scored need to ensure that the reader recalls the information presented as she is about to determine a score. Creatively infusing facts and figures into a piece of writing can give those bits of information the necessary staying power to be remembered at the end of the reading.

What do you have to know?

Acknowledge that a fact or statistic stated creatively has a better chance of being remembered than one that is just stated.

Take this frightening fact extracted from my morning newspaper:

> In my county, 23% of high school juniors are deemed ready for college-level English.[1]

By itself, the fact is startling, but it can have still greater staying power if we accessorize it, utilizing some rhetorical strategies previously practiced in Lesson 16.

1. How about employing **a rhetorical question** to emphasize the startling nature of the fact?

    Is it possible that you could have a 3.5 GPA in college prep courses and still not be prepared for college? Not only is it possible—in my county, it's more than likely. Seventy-seven percent of high school juniors are ineligible for college-level English according to a California State University study.

Note how the rhetorical question illustrates with a compelling specific example and how the 23 percent is translated into 77 percent to emphasize the failure rate. Also note that mentioning the source of the statistic adds credibility to your argument. These rhetorical ploys add persuasive impact and sear the fact into the reader's memory.

2. Let's try another strategy: **translating the statistic into a literal—but unrealistic—extension:**

    Imagine if only 7 people in your high school English class were actually being prepared for college—the other 23 were merely wasting their time. Well, according to a recent study by the California State University system, this is not that far from the truth. Only 23 percent of high school juniors in my county were deemed ready for college-level English.

When the statistic is translated into a relatable extension, it becomes personal. The reader is forced to imagine his high school classmates doomed to a stagnant school experience devoid of meaningful instruction.

---

1. Kerry Benefield, "Half of CSU Freshmen Lack Skills for College Courses," *The Press Democrat,* July 20, 2010. A1-9. Print.

3. We could also try an **analogy**—using the fact to make a hypothetical compari-
    son with another situation:
    Graduating students from high school ill-prepared to face college-level Eng-
    lish classes is like promoting students from beginning swim lessons to
    advanced—kids are going to drown. According to a recent study by the Cali-
    fornia State University system, a mere 23 percent of high school juniors in my
    county were deemed ready for college-level English—that's a lot of kids who
    will be struggling to stay afloat in their college composition courses.

Perhaps an image of students struggling to stay afloat amidst a sea of textbooks
and papers comes to mind; regardless, the analogy assists readers who may be
removed from the school experience a chance to understand the essential argument
by making the comparison to a much more common experience—swim lessons.

What do you have to do?

Strive to creatively infuse facts into your writing. Experiment with the three strategies illustrated previously. Or, if you have a creative brain surge, try one of your own
strategies to make a fact more memorable.

Use different strategies to creatively express the following facts and stats. Each fact
is linked to a topic area to give you an idea of how to focus your writing.

Topic: poverty
Fact: Children growing up in poverty will eventually cost the U.S. economy
$500 billion.

Topic: money
Fact: Five percent of Americans qualify as compulsive shoppers, with men
and women being equally represented in their numbers.

Topic: diversity
Fact: The new U.S. Congress has a record number of women, a record number of Buddhists, and a record number of Muslims.

Topic: fairness
Fact : Only 25 of the 535 members of Congress have come under fire in
combat.

Topic: childhood obesity
Fact: Chinese children are on average 2.5 inches taller and 6.6 pounds heavier than they were 30 years ago.

Topic: photography
Fact: The most requested document from the National Archives is the photo of Elvis Presley shaking hands with President Nixon.

HINT

If you'd like further practice infusing facts creatively, two great places to get the random facts are: Harper's Index online: http://www.harpers.org/subjects/ HarpersIndex and the "Noted" section of the weekly news magazine, *The Week*. Online you can access this portion of the magazine at: http://www.theweekdaily. com/sub_section/index/cartoons_wit/noted.

29. Beg to Differ—or Not: Arguing in Three Sentences Without Begging the Question

Begging the question is repeating a claim without providing a warrant or reason and certainly no supporting examples. Unfortunately, begging the question is a dominant fallacy in most high school students' writing. I've theorized it's because we teachers have encouraged you to do it.

In classes where teachers merely check in homework without reading it or award points for completed assignments regardless of the answers, adroit students get very good at repeating themselves using slightly different words to fill in the blank space or respond to questions they haven't prepared for.

Here is an example of the crime of begging the question—in a short paragraph that attempts to explain begging the question:

> Begging the question is prevalent among college-bound high school students. Many students beg the question in their college-prep courses. It is not uncommon for juniors and seniors planning to attend universities to employ the technique of begging the question.

Notice how the above three sentences repeat the same claim, using slightly different words, without providing a reason why or a supporting example. This shotgun blast of words may be rewarded on a high school homework assignment, but it's sniper fire precision that you need for on demand writing.

In this lesson, you'll come to recognize and remedy begging the question in your own writing and receive a checklist to help you tailor your arguments to be brief yet logical.

Why should you care?

In on demand writing situations, you can't afford to beg the question. You need word economy; and, most important, you need to be certain your words are saying something!

What do you have to know?

First, be willing to admit that you've relied on begging the question when you felt you had to fill the blank space on an exam or in response to an essay prompt.

Begging the question is really repeating yourself but using different words to do so. You provide no examples and no reasons, but you do provide a bunch of words! To help you detect begging the question, read the sample three-sentence arguments made in response to an essay that questioned whether classic literature should be taught in high schools. Note the differences between the Good, Bad, and Fluffy responses.

Sample Claim (extracted from Joan Ryan's "Life Lessons on the Living Room Shelf" in the *San Francisco Chronicle*, February 25, 1996):

"Only 24 percent [of high school teachers] considered classic literature essential."

The Good

If something is essential, one can't live life without it. Few would argue that students could survive in today's brisk-paced world without an understanding of economics, technology know-how, and crisp communication skills. Knowing the name of Romeo's cousin or being able to recite Chaucer's prologue to *The Canterbury Tales* might come in handy in a hot game of Trivial Pursuit, but knowledge of classical literature is not a prerequisite for life.

> This paragraph succinctly states its position, moves on to explain why other skills are more essential, and finally uses specific concrete illustrations to illustrate the original argument. It definitely does not beg the question.

The Bad

It's not like anyone is forcing you to read anything terrible. If somone wants to read something other than classical literature, they can read it when they want to. It's not like their teachers can control what they read, they are not that powerful.

Everything's wrong. Not only is it a vague, unsupported, illogical argument, but it mixes and matches pronouns (one/they/you) and suffers from pronoun agreement problems (someone/they). The paragraph also sports a comma splice in the last sentence, making it four ugly sentences too long.

The Fluffy

I disagree with the English teachers who think that classical literature is no longer essential. It is important that all of us be forced to read certain books in high school that we wouldn't otherwise pick up and read on our own. If high schools do not make us read the classics, then who will make sure we read these important books?

This paragraph repeats the same arguments without offering proof or a reason. It "begs the question." It also states the obvious, "I disagree." By assuming "all" students are the same, it generates a "sweeping generalization" fallacy. It also wastes 1 of its 3 sentences asking a question rather than offering an example or a reason to support its argument.

Your Goal—When asked to agree or disagree with an article or excerpt—as in the case of ACT style prompts—strive to avoid begging the question and using blantantly obvious phrasing. Most important, remember that your response should be a self-contained argument that asserts a claim, supports it, and concludes by addressing what we should do or think.

What do you have to do?

To ensure when asked to confirm or challenge a position that you are actually formulating a meaningful argument, try crafting three-sentence replies to an author's argument. Ideally this will assist you in assessing your own logical development and discovering for yourself that being specific with an example is probably the best protection against fallacy and the best guarantee that your argument is cogent.

As you read an essay or article, get in the practice of "reading with a pencil," marking lines or phrases that strike a nerve or compel you to disagree. It doesn't matter if you're reading the sports page or a fashion magazine; keep that pencil in your hand. After you've finished an article, select a line or phrase that really gets your dander up. Challenge yourself to dismantle the author's argument in only three sentences—then run those sentences through the checklist to test for logic. You'll find that it's much easier to scrutinize three sentences than an entire essay, and you'll be more inclined to be more critical and to do more reworking.

Or opt to choose three quotations from Appendix 1 and respond to them in three-sentence arguments.

Checklist Test for Logical and Accurate Paragraphs

_____   Have you avoided sweeping generalizations? (e.g., "Every . . .", "All . . .", "Always . . .", etc.)

_____   Have you offered a specific supporting example?

_____   Have you supported assertions with reasons? (e.g., Why is this the case?)

_____   Have you sniffed out the B.O.? (e.g., I agree, I think, I feel, In my opinion . . .)

_____   Have you avoided the pronoun "you"?

_____   Have you caught run-on sentences? (Check that what appear on either side of a comma are not two independent clauses.)

30. The Rhetorical Mode Scavenger Hunt: Reading Prose Like a Pro

If you haven't already been exposed to the term "rhetorical mode" in your English class—it's a term that refers to an author's organizational pattern. An author may organize her ideas in a compare-contrast pattern or perhaps a cause-and-effect format. When you write a persuasive essay with a qualified thesis acknowledging your opposition, you're more than likely writing in a classical argument pattern; if you're asked to explore how something came to be the way it is, you're probably penning a process-analysis essay. Odds are that you've been using rhetorical modes and just not calling them such.

Popular magazines and nonacademic publications are great resources for finding an abundance of rhetorical modes. For instance, if I want my students to read a process-and-analysis essay, other than the tired one in our writing textbook, I rifle through my daughter's fashion magazines—although it's unlikely that I'll ever be able to top the article extracted by one of my students for his scavenger hunt project, "How to Walk Like a Prom Queen"—taken from his sister's *Seventeen* magazine. Ironically, the student was running for prom king that year, and his paragraph of analysis provided hysterical tongue-in-cheek enthusiasm for his topic.

My favorite part of the newspaper is the sports page. Yet, with the exception of a once-a-year outing to a baseball game, I am not a sports fan. I am a fan, however, of good writing. Sportswriters have to be especially creative since for them only the names and the dates change; some teams win and others lose—the story stays the same. Their job as writers is to make those stories fresh and interesting every day. That's why I read the sports page. Vivid narratives, creative analogies, original organizational patterns abound. If I'm looking for a sample comparison-contrast essay to share with a class, the first place I turn is the sports page; if I'm looking for a division or classification essay, to the sports section I go.

In this lesson, you will receive an overview of the various rhetorical modes; you'll be encouraged to scavenge for examples of these organizational patterns in your favorite print media, and then you'll be coached on how to construct a précis or concise summary of the works.

Why should you care?

Analytical reading is demanded on most high-stakes tests like the SAT and AP exams. Often you are expected to read an entire essay and offer a full-length analytical essay in return. Coming to understand some of the different ways writers organize arguments for impact is a sophisticated step in the composition process. Furthermore, exposing you to the various organizational patterns of essays will prepare you for your basic college composition course.

What do you have to know?

Recall in Chapter Four when you were coached on how to dissect on demand writing prompts for key verbs that indicated how you should respond to the prompt. Key words like "narrate" or "evaluate" also direct you to use a particular organizational pattern or mode. The modes you'd be most likely asked to demonstrate in an on demand writing situation are: classical argument, personal narrative, evaluative, and cause and effect. See the following chart for the prompt stem verbs that signal a particular mode or organizational pattern. Then go to *Rhetorical Modes and Their Criteria* below to learn more about using them.

If the prompt stem verbs are . . .	Your essay should . . .	Follow the mode of . . .
Agree or disagree	take a stance and use persuasive language.	classical argument
Confirm, challenge, or qualify	acknowledge the opposition, but still take a stance and use persuasive language.	classical argument
Describe a time when	narrate a detailed story that supports an assertion.	personal narrative
Evaluate	weigh the pros and cons or the harms and benefits, but ultimately conclude by determining to what degree the subject is good or beneficial.	evaluative

Explain why	explore the causes of an event or speculate on the causes and effects of a policy change.	cause and effect

To find models of these rhetorical modes in real essays, type the name of the mode and the phrase "rhetorical mode" (e.g., "evaluative rhetorical mode") into a Google search; the search engine will direct you to a variety of college writing websites where you can view representative samples of the various modes. Most college composition courses require students to purchase a reader—or collection of essays that are organized by rhetorical mode. You can probably find a used composition reader online or at a local bookstore. I'd recommend *Subject and Strategy: A Rhetoric Reader* or *The Riverside Reader*.

To begin, read what you want—hunting for articles in old newspapers and magazines. When you find an article that captures your interest, read it; then see if you can identify its mode using the criteria provided below. Do not be surprised if you encounter pieces that blend more than one mode. This is quite common among published pieces of writing that have had the luxury of being composed in more than 30–45 minutes!

HINT

Due to the ease with which online sources will help you catalogue rhetorical modes without you having to be able to identify them, to truly appreciate how these organizational patterns abound it's best to hunt for articles on old magazines and newspapers. Dirtying your hands with newsprint is the best way to assure that you are testing your knowledge of how arguments are constructed. Of course, if you don't have access to print media or you can't resist the allure of the *New York Times* online, you can use your favorite online magazine or newspaper to test your recognition of rhetorical patterns.

In your search for articles that demonstrate different rhetorical modes, beware: news stories are not rhetorical. The articles you clip must have a thesis (implied or stated) being asserted. You may be tempted to deem a news story a cause-and-effect essay because it offers potential causes or effects (e.g., "Why You'll Be Paying More at the Pump This Summer"). Know that news stories contain a balance of expert opinion—in other words, the arguments are attributed to people other than the author. To ensure that you're reading and analyzing persuasion only, stay away from the front-page news section and veer more toward the editorial pages and review sections. As for my favorite section, the sports page, look for the local or syndicated columnists. They usually have a picture accompanying their byline. Being able to distinguish persuasion from news analysis in the media is the underlying goal of this exercise!

Rhetorical Modes and Their Criteria

1. CAUSE/EFFECT

The function of a cause-and-effect essay may be to emphasize the speculation of causes *and/or* effects.

In a cause-and-effect essay, the writer . . .

- May choose to emphasize causes, attempting to explain *why*?
- May choose to emphasize effects, attempting to explain consequences (usually future or long term).
- May organize the argument a "causal chain" in which a cause makes an effect, which makes another effect, etc.
- Must acknowledge other possible causes and/or effects to avoid causal fallacy or faulty logic.

2. CLASSICAL ARGUMENT

The function of a classical argument is to promote a position with a balance of logic and emotion while acknowledging prominent opposition.

In a classical argument, the writer . . .

- Asserts a thesis, then proves it with subsequent claims and supporting detail.

- May employ emotional arguments (pathos) *and/or* logical arguments (logos).
- May establish his credibility (ethos) by citing personal experience or with research or other evidence.
- Organizes the argument using either deductive or inductive reasoning.
- Concludes by moving beyond the initial thesis.

3. CLASSIFICATION

The function of a classification essay is to sort items into categories — usually to point out never-before-considered similarities or differences.

In a classification essay, the writer . . .

- Sorts items into categories (e.g., my students can be classified as scholars, smooth talkers, and slackers). The categories should be:
  - consistent and mutually exclusive
  - account for all the members of your subject class
- Asserts a thesis by the conclusion of the essay (e.g., only the scholars will pass the final exam).

4. COMPARISON/CONTRAST

The function of a comparison/contrast essay is to clarify or reach some conclusion about the subjects being compared or contrasted.

In a classical argument, the writer . . .

- Points out similarities *and/or* differences between two or more subjects from the same class or category (e.g., two ballplayers or two musicians).
- May organize the information either using the point-by-point method *or* block format.
  - In the point-by-point method, the attributes of both subjects are discussed one by one (e.g., the musicians' natural talent, their impact on their genre, and the quality of their concerts). In the point-by-point method, internal conclusions about the subjects are drawn throughout the essay.
  - In the block format, one subject is discussed first, then the second (e.g., one musician is thoroughly discussed before a small transition segues to the other musician's attributes). In the block format, the essay hinges on the impact of the concluding paragraph.

5. DEFINITION

The function of a definition essay is to define or redefine a word, idea, trend, or personality.

In a definition essay, the writer . . .

- Must employ other modes within the essay (e.g., examples, description, comparison/contrast) to achieve her purpose.
- Usually organizes the material inductively—reasoning through specific examples then moving to a general conclusion.
- May state or imply a thesis through tone and diction.

6. DIVISION

The function of a division essay is to assert a thesis about the subject under discussion by focusing on a few key subunits.

In a division essay, the writer . . .

- Breaks down a single large unit into smaller subunits (e.g., a scholar is comprised of diligence, intelligence, and stress).
- Divides the subject selectively—the writer need not acknowledge *all* of the subject's subunits (e.g., scholars may also be good looking, but this point detracts from my thesis).
- States or implies a thesis but emphasizes it in the conclusion.

7. EVALUATIVE

The function of an evaluative essay is to assess the effectiveness or merit of a subject.

In an evaluative essay, the writer . . .

- Uses set criteria to assess the subject.
- Employs specific examples to support claims.
- Implies a thesis through tone—the attitude portrayed toward the subject.
- Establishes credibility as an evaluator by demonstrating knowledge of the subject.
- Dines with the opposing viewpoint.

8. EXAMPLE/ILLUSTRATION

The function of an example essay is to enhance a generalization. (e.g., students who are passive don't learn) by illustrating with specific examples (e.g., several examples of passive students who failed to learn).

In an example or illustration essay, the writer . . .

- Colors examples with rich sensory detail and vivid verbs.
- Organizes examples based on their impact, with the strongest usually saved for last.
- Reveals in the conclusion the full thesis, which moves beyond the generalization (e.g., passive students endanger their future).

9. PERSONAL NARRATIVE/REFLECTIVE

The function of a personal narrative or reflective essay is to use personal experience as a means for asserting a position on a larger issue.

In a personal narrative essay, the writer . . .

- Illustrates an autobiographical story with specific sensory detail and may include dialogue.
- Sequences events clearly with time markers such as "next" or "then."
- May provide context, describing background incidents, setting, or people.
- Establishes tone—an attitude toward the subject being described—through apt choice of words.
- Implies thesis through details and tone.
- Pauses to muse about the retrospective significance of the event(s) if it's a reflective essay.

10. PROCESS ANALYSIS

The function of a process-analysis essay may be to assert something about the nature of a process or to advocate a change in a process.

In a process-analysis essay, the writer . . .

- Emphasizes the process or the analysis of a subject depending on the author's intent.

- Sequences events clearly with time markers such as "next" or "then."
- Encourages the reader to take part in the process being described by using the informal pronoun "you."
- Implies a thesis through tone, which is conveyed through the details.

Note: Unless a thesis is being suggested, a process analysis is merely a recipe.

11. SATIRE

The function of satire is to unseat traditional arguments by using shock tactics intended to make an audience rethink an issue.

In a satire, the writer . . .
- Establishes credibility with research or evidence.
- Employs effective exaggeration.
- Maintains control by one or more of the following means . . .
  - *Not* employing only attack and abuse
  - Preserving logic
  - Using highbrow diction and tone
- Advocates reform (e.g., "A Modest Proposal").

Note: An essay with a satirical tone may only mock its topic, but a true *satire* advocates change.

What do you have to do?

Locate a few articles that demonstrate various organizational patterns or modes and strive to paraphrase the author's argument. To rhetorically analyze an article, do the following:

- explain *why* the article is a particular mode
- reference specific criteria for that rhetorical mode

- locate at least one quote from the article as proof of its mode
- indicate the author's purpose
- establish a link between the author's purpose and the mode (answer the question, "How did this mode enhance the author's purpose?")

The last item—connecting the author's purpose to his choice of rhetorical mode—is the most essential part of rhetorical analysis. If you do nothing else, endeavor to make this connection as you read your favorite sports columnist or film reviewer.

31. The Rhetorical Précis: Paraphrasing with Precision

Many on demand writing exams, such as the ACT, ask you to first paraphrase an author's position or point of view as expressed in a brief article before agreeing or disagreeing with that position. Essentially what's being requested is a rhetorical précis.

A rhetorical précis is a concise summary that focuses on the author's argument. A précis can be constructed based on a formula and has four distinct components that, if included, will ensure that you've not only summarized the author's argument but made a meaningful connection to the position you plan to take in your own essay.

What do you have to know?

Since your ultimate goal is to compose a persuasive essay, you need to be careful not to devote too much time or ink when a prompt asks you to first provide a summary of an article. The following four-sentence template can come in handy for creating a concise, meaningful paraphrase.[2]

Template of a Rhetorical Précis

Sentence 1: Name of author, genre, and title of work; a rhetorically accurate verb (e.g., "claims," "speculates," "evaluates") and a *that clause* containing the major assertion or thesis of the work being summarized.

---

2. The précis template is a hybrid of a similar formula found in the book *Reading Rhetorically* by John C. Bean.

Sentence 2: A chronological explanation of how the author supports the thesis.

Sentence 3: Specific supporting example(s) that you find compelling.

Sentence 4: Discuss the effect of the mode on the intended audience, followed by an "in order to" phrase that addresses the author's purpose.

The most significant sentence of the rhetorical précis is the last one—note how you are expected to link the rhetorical mode to the author's purpose. Read the following student samples to appreciate how a rhetorical précis is crafted.

Sample Rhetorical Précis

CAUSE AND EFFECT

In his sports column, "Giants Built to Pitch, But Defense Looks a Little Shaky," Lowell Cohn employs the mode of cause and effect to claim that the San Francisco Giants baseball team is supposed to be a defensive team, but they are currently utilizing great pitching and lacking good fielding. The author first describes the recent game and how the Giants' fielding failed, moves on to the problem this presents in all games, and finishes by pointing out the specific fielders who are bringing the team down. When Cohn begins bashing individual players with "So now's the time for brutal honesty," he transitions into specific examples which lends credibility to his argument. Lowell Cohn emphasizes the causes that will lead to an effect, in order to convince readers that Giants' bad fielding will lead to their demise this season.

EVALUATIVE

In his restaurant review, "Silvers' Fine Eats," Jeff Cox evaluates the price, food, and atmosphere of Jackson's Bar and Oven to suggest that the restaurant is relaxed and homelike with simple food. Cox first describes the history of the restaurant, then the layout, and finally the food, evaluating each and describing the positive qualities in order to persuade the reader to try Jackson's Bar and Oven. When describing the House made Cheesy Spaetzle, "Spaetzle are tiny dumplings just made for soaking up rich brown German meat sauces, and they lose purpose served by themselves," Cox acknowledges his opposition by criticizing the dish and how it is out of place, thus establishing his ethos by straying from his constant praise. Cox provides clear criteria for his evaluation while providing historical information, knowledge about food origin, and acknowledging his opposition in order to convince people to eat at Jackson's Bar and Oven.[3]

What do you have to do?

Practice plugging into the précis template when asked to summarize an author's argument for an on demand essay prompt. Consider the sample ACT prompt found in Appendix 6 as a starting place.

Read the student sample essays responding to the prompt and gauge the success of their paraphrase of the author's argument using the guidelines for a rhetorical précis. You'll find that the high-scoring essay employed a precise paragraph of paraphrase very close to that of the rhetorical précis model.

---

3. Lowell Cohn, "Giants Built to Pitch, But Defense Looks a Little Shaky," *The Press Democrat*, March 14, 2010. Print; Jeff Cox, "Silvers' Fine Eats," *The Press Democrat*, March 21, 2010. Print.

Appendixes

Appendix 1: Prompts for Practice

For practice in crafting qualified thesis statements, roadmapping, or writing essays, here is a list of notable quotations with which you can agree, disagree, or qualify.

"Don't offer me advice, give me money."—Spanish proverb

"Many receive advice, only the wise profit by it."—Syrus

"Success for the striver washes away the effort of striving."—Pindar

"Riches are for spending."—Francis Bacon

"What you don't see with your eyes, don't invent with your tongue."—Jewish proverb

"Laws go where dollars please."—Portuguese proverb

"One sword keeps another in the sheath."—George Herbert

"No one is more profoundly sad than he who laughs too much."—Jean Paul Richter

"Failure changes us for the better, success for the worse."—Seneca

"The language of friendship is not words, but meanings."—Henry David Thoreau

"The magic of first love is our ignorance that it can never end."—Disraeli

"A man is judged by his deeds, not by his words."—Russian proverb

"Talent is most likely to be found among dissenters and rebels."—David Ogilvy

"Great ideas often receive violent opposition from mediocre minds."—Albert Einstein

"If you live in the river, you should make friends with the crocodile."—Indian proverb

"If you obey all of the rules, you miss all of the fun."—Katharine Hepburn

"If you would persuade, you must appeal to interest rather than intellect."—Ben Franklin

"You can't shake hands with a closed fist."—Golda Meier

"The past is the best prophet of the future."—Lord Byron

"A room without books is like a body without a soul."—Cicero

"A proverb is a short sentence based on long experience."—Miguel de Cervantes

Appendix 2: 6-Point Scoring Guide for the SAT*

Essay Scoring Guide

The Scoring Guide addresses critical thinking, development of ideas, organization, vocabulary, sentence structure, and mechanics.

Score of 6

An essay in this category is *outstanding*, demonstrating *clear and consistent mastery*, although it may have a few minor errors. A typical essay

- effectively and insightfully develops a point of view on the issue and demonstrates outstanding critical thinking, using clearly appropriate examples, reasons, and other evidence to support its position

- is well organized and clearly focused, demonstrating clear coherence and smooth progression of ideas

- exhibits skillful use of language, using a varied, accurate, and apt vocabulary

- demonstrates meaningful variety in sentence structure

- is free of most errors in grammar, usage, and mechanics

Score of 5

An essay in this category is *effective*, demonstrating *reasonably consistent mastery*, although it will have occasional errors or lapses in quality. A typical essay

- effectively develops a point of view on the issue and demonstrates strong critical thinking, generally using appropriate examples, reasons, and other evidence to support its position

---

*Educational Testing Service. SAT Reasoning Test. "Essay Scoring Guide" 2004. 25 July 2008. <http://www.collegeboard.com/student/testing/sat/about/sat/essay_scoring.html>

SAT test materials selected from the SAT Reasoning Test reprinted by permission of the College Board, the copyright owner.

Permission to reprint SAT materials does not constitute review or endorsement by Educational Testing Service or the College Board of this publication as a whole or of any other questions or testing information it may contain.

- is well organized and focused, demonstrating coherence and progression of ideas
- exhibits facility in the use of language, using appropriate vocabulary
- demonstrates variety in sentence structure
- is generally free of most errors in grammar, usage, and mechanics

Score of 4

An essay in this category is *competent*, demonstrating *adequate mastery*, although it will have lapses in quality. A typical essay

- develops a point of view on the issue and demonstrates competent critical thinking, using adequate examples, reasons, and other evidence to support its position
- is generally organized and focused, demonstrating some coherence and progression of ideas
- exhibits adequate but inconsistent facility in the use of language, using generally appropriate vocabulary
- demonstrates some variety in sentence structure
- has some errors in grammar, usage, and mechanics

Score of 3

An essay in this category is *inadequate*, but demonstrates *developing mastery*, and is marked by ONE OR MORE of the following weaknesses:

- develops a point of view on the issue, demonstrating some critical thinking, but may do so inconsistently or use inadequate examples, reasons, or other evidence to support its position
- is limited in its organization or focus, or may demonstrate some lapses in coherence or progression of ideas
- displays developing facility in the use of language, but sometimes uses weak vocabulary or inappropriate word choice
- lacks variety or demonstrates problems in sentence structure
- contains an accumulation of errors in grammar, usage, and mechanics

Score of 2

An essay in this category is *seriously limited*, demonstrating *little mastery*, and is flawed by ONE OR MORE of the following weaknesses:

- develops a point of view on the issue that is vague or seriously limited, demonstrating weak critical thinking, providing inappropriate or insufficient examples, reasons, or other evidence to support its position

- is poorly organized and/or focused, or demonstrates serious problems with coherence or progression of ideas

- displays very little facility in the use of language, using very limited vocabulary or incorrect word choice

- demonstrates frequent problems in sentence structure

- contains errors in grammar, usage, and mechanics so serious that meaning is somewhat obscured

Score of 1

An essay in this category is *fundamentally lacking*, demonstrating *very little or no mastery*, and is severely flawed by ONE OR MORE of the following weaknesses:

- develops no viable point of view on the issue, or provides little or no evidence to support its position

- is disorganized or unfocused, resulting in a disjointed or incoherent essay

- displays fundamental errors in vocabulary

- demonstrates severe flaws in sentence structure

- contains pervasive errors in grammar, usage, or mechanics that persistently interfere with meaning

Score of 0

Students will receive a score of zero if they do not write an essay, if their essay is not written on the essay assignment, or if the essay is deemed illegible after several attempts have been made to read and score it.

Appendix 3: Sample Student Essays on a 25-minute SAT Prompt

Use these essays in conjunction with Lesson 20 "Students as Peer Coaches: Scoring Other Students' Essays."

These essays were written in class (yes, their errors are intact) on the following 25-minute SAT prompt:

> *The Roman philosopher Seneca once said: "Failure changes us for the better."*
> *Plan and write an essay in which you agree, disagree, or qualify the above*
> *aphorism. Support your position with reasoning and examples taken from*
> *your reading, studies, experiences, or observations.*

The essays were then T-scored by fellow students. You'll find their scores in Appendix 4.

JM: Sample Essay

IPODs Don't Fall In Toilets For No Reason

Michael Jordan once said, "My failures have taught me how to succeed." Michael Jordan is arguably the most successful basketball player ever to play the game, but he has also failed much more than the average basketball player. Although some would say that failure does not help, I disagree because failure shows an individual his or her flaws and helps that person to change their ways.

Failure creates better people because it humbles people. My friend Jerry is a great baseball player. I've played baseball with him ever since we were little. He used to be a real trash-talker, He would always tell the players on the other team how he was gonna get them out and that there was no way that they would get on base. Awhile back, In our semi-final game, we were up by one run and there was one out and it was the last inning. He was talking more than usual this game. There was a lot of pressure because the bases were loaded. There was a grounder up the right side and the second baseman got it and tossed it to Jerry at second. He grabbed it for the out at second and threw it at first to turn two, but the ball stuck in his hand for just a split second. He threw the ball in the dirt and two unearned runs ended up scoring; when the game should have been over. We lost. From that moment on, Jerry has not talked one word of trash. He also seems to play better now as well; because he us more focused on the game and not just in getting into the other team's heads.

Failure teaches us more lessons than succeeding does. Recently, I dropped my IPOD in the toilet and it is now broken. I had it wedged in between my boxers and my stomach. Somehow it ended up getting in the air and I was frantically grasping for it with both hands. I looked like a fire juggler who started his trick and then realized that he actually couldn't handle the fire torches. Then it fell through both my hands and PLUNCK! It fell straight into the toilet. I failed to protect my IPOD. Since I have decided to not only groan and pout about the incident, I've learned something from it. Now I have the story and not only can I learn from this experience so that I never drop a valuable in the toilet, but I can tell others; to prevent them from using valuables while near the toilet.

Failure makes us better people, but success teaches us nothing. So then how is failure failing? Failure is only failing if we do not learn anything from the incident, if I didn't learn anything from dropping my IPOD into the toilet, then I would have failed. I succeeded however because I learned something from the experience. Failure teaches us great lessons and helps us to live out greater more knowledgeable lives. Failure is the reason for success, so we should all open our eyes and learn from our mistakes.

PC Sample Essay

Bloody Knuckles

I was 13 years old, at the time in seventh grade, a period where popularity reigned supreme and the hierarchy of "cool" was the only thing on my young little mind. At my particular middle school recess time was entirely dominated by one activity if you wanted to be cool you had to get good at that game; the game of bloody knuckles. I was not a particularly physical kid, I would have preferred to play Stratego or Risk, but nonetheless I had the strong desire to be cool so on a bright sunny day when the group of cool kids asked me to join them I was very excited. Shortly after I realized that my excitement was a false hope as I was brutally maimed by the joyfull crowd of cool boys. However out of this abismol failure I took new resolve to find my own identity and pursue a better game. Although failure can lead people through hard times the lessons learned will benefit you infinitely.

Al Gore learned this lesson in the 2000 election when his victory was wretched from his hands by the electoral college system. It was this resolve that lead him to the winning of a nobel prize.

During the early 1900's America experienced a period of depression called the great depression. However out of this era came a strong leader. Franklin D. Roosevelt whose New Deal policy is a standard for the worlds industrial policy. While failure may make life a little cumbersome it is this hard work that gives us the necessary lessons to do great. We should look at failure not as an end all be all of our existence and take it rather as an opportunity to succeed.

EN Sample Essay

Yay! I Failed!

It is commonly known that everyone learns from their mistakes. Although failure may sometimes seem so extreme and embarassing to actually be positive, it is nevertheless a trigger for comparison between success and failure, improvement, and therefore a means of change.

Sometimes the humiliation of failure may seem to be the focus of the situation. In terms of embarrassment, recently resigned governor of New York, Eliot Spitzer, was caught engaging with a prostitute after dutifully rallying for morality for years. Although it may seem that his life, career, and family are over, he still has some hope. He can take his failure and change.

Perfect is boring. Not being a failure once in a while causes no substance in a personality. As a child, I was often called miss perfect, and I hated it. It gave no room for me to improve. Therefore, being failing is a way to compare the good and the bad.

After comparing being a failure with success, it is easy to reflect, and change. After doing horribly on an AP exam one year, but then scoring a 5 the next year, it is easy to reflect on what was improved, and try to focus on remaining consistent in success. Failure betters the world by allowing people to change to improve.

Failure brings variety and variety is a means of comparison which leaves room for improvement. Failure is nothing to be ashamed of and should be accepted in our society as a tool for comparison, change, and improvement.

Appendix 4: Scores of Sample Student Essays on a 25-minute SAT Prompt

JM (high score)

1st reader

+	6	–
Vivid supporting examples! Strong critical thinking Well-drawn conclusion		A few slips in grammar

2nd reader

+	6	–
Great examples! Loved the title! Focused!		Could use more variety in sentence structure

PC (low score)

1st reader

+	2	–
Funny! Clear thesis		Could be more focused Needs more examples Draw a conclusion

2nd reader

+	3	−
Good viewpoint		Could develop thesis more
Some examples		Provide more analysis of examples
		Points could be linked together more

EN (middle score)

1st reader

+	4	−
Clear response to the prompt		Repetitive reasons
Adequate examples		Too many subject/verb agreement errors
Well organized		
Clear critical thinking		

2nd reader

+	4	−
Well-developed thesis		Several awkward sentences
Good examples		Intro a bit confusing

Appendix 5: Scoring Guidelines for the ACT Exam*

These are the descriptions of scoring criteria that the trained readers will follow to determine the score (1–6) for your essay. Papers at each level exhibit *all* or *most* of the characteristics described at each score point.

Score = 6

Essays within this score range demonstrate effective skill in responding to the task.

The essay shows a clear understanding of the task. The essay takes a position on the issue and may offer a critical context for discussion. The essay addresses complexity by examining different perspectives on the issue, or by evaluating the implications and/or complications of the issue, or by fully responding to counterarguments to the writer's position. Development of ideas is ample, specific, and logical. Most ideas are fully elaborated. A clear focus on the specific issue in the prompt is maintained. The organization of the essay is clear: the organization may be somewhat predictable or it may grow from the writer's purpose. Ideas are logically sequenced. Most transitions reflect the writer's logic and are usually integrated into the essay. The introduction and conclusion are effective, clear, and well developed. The essay shows a good command of language. Sentences are varied and word choice is varied and precise. There are few, if any, errors to distract the reader.

Score = 5

Essays within this score range demonstrate competent skill in responding to the task.

The essay shows a clear understanding of the task. The essay takes a position on the issue and may offer a broad context for discussion. The essay shows recognition of complexity by partially evaluating the implications and/or complications of the issue, or by responding to counterarguments to the writer's position. Development of ideas is specific and logical. Most ideas are elaborated, with clear movement between general statements and specific reasons, examples, and details. Focus on the specific issue in the prompt is maintained. The organization of the essay is clear, although it may be predictable. Ideas are logically sequenced, although simple and

*"Scoring Guidelines" for the ACT Exam. 2008: http://www.actstudent.org/writing/scores/guidelines.html . 27 August 2008. Reproduced with permission.

obvious transitions may be used. The introduction and conclusion are clear and generally well developed. Language is competent. Sentences are somewhat varied and word choice is sometimes varied and precise. There may be a few errors, but they are rarely distracting.

Score = 4

Essays within this score range demonstrate adequate skill in responding to the task.

The essay shows an understanding of the task. The essay takes a position on the issue and may offer some context for discussion. The essay may show some recognition of complexity by providing some response to counterarguments to the writer's position. Development of ideas is adequate, with some movement between general statements and specific reasons, examples, and details. Focus on the specific issue in the prompt is maintained throughout most of the essay. The organization of the essay is apparent but predictable. Some evidence of logical sequencing of ideas is apparent, although most transitions are simple and obvious. The introduction and conclusion are clear and somewhat developed. Language is adequate, with some sentence variety and appropriate word choice. There may be some distracting errors, but they do not impede understanding.

Score = 3

Essays within this score range demonstrate some developing skill in responding to the task.

The essay shows some understanding of the task. The essay takes a position on the issue but does not offer a context for discussion. The essay may acknowledge a counterargument to the writer's position, but its development is brief or unclear. Development of ideas is limited and may be repetitious, with little, if any, movement between general statements and specific reasons, examples, and details. Focus on the general topic is maintained, but focus on the specific issue in the prompt may not be maintained. The organization of the essay is simple. Ideas are logically grouped within parts of the essay, but there is little or no evidence of logical sequencing of ideas. Transitions, if used, are simple and obvious. An introduction and conclusion are clearly discernible but underdeveloped. Language shows a basic control. Sentences show a little variety and word choice is appropriate. Errors may be distracting and may occasionally impede understanding.

Score = 2
Essays within this score range demonstrate inconsistent or weak skill in responding to the task.

The essay shows a weak understanding of the task. The essay may not take a position on the issue, or the essay may take a position but fail to convey reasons to support that position, or the essay may take a position but fail to maintain a stance. There is little or no recognition of a counterargument to the writer's position. The essay is thinly developed. If examples are given, they are general and may not be clearly relevant. The essay may include extensive repetition of the writer's ideas or of ideas in the prompt. Focus on the general topic is maintained, but focus on the specific issue in the prompt may not be maintained. There is some indication of an organizational structure, and some logical grouping of ideas within parts of the essay is apparent. Transitions, if used, are simple and obvious, and they may be inappropriate or misleading. An introduction and conclusion are discernible but minimal. Sentence structure and word choice are usually simple. Errors may be frequently distracting and may sometimes impede understanding.

Score = 1
Essays within this score range show little or no skill in responding to the task.

The essay shows little or no understanding of the task. If the essay takes a position, it fails to convey reasons to support that position. The essay is minimally developed. The essay may include excessive repetition of the writer's ideas or of ideas in the prompt. Focus on the general topic is usually maintained, but focus on the specific issue in the prompt may not be maintained. There is little or no evidence of an organizational structure or of the logical grouping of ideas. Transitions are rarely used. If present, an introduction and conclusion are minimal. Sentence structure and word choice are simple. Errors may be frequently distracting and may significantly impede understanding.

No Score
Blank, Off-Topic, Illegible, Not in English, or Void.

Appendix 6: Sample Student Essays on a 30-minute ACT Prompt

Use these essays in conjunction with Lesson 20 "Students as Peer Coaches: Scoring Other Students' Essays."

These essays were written in class (yes, their errors are intact) on the following 30-minute ACT-style prompt:

Read the following editorial and respond to the prompt that follows in a well-reasoned essay.

> I spent quite a bit of time alone as a teenager, licking my latest social wound, brooding over the meaning of life, mooning over Connie or Marie of Carole. (At one point, I recall, I was besotted with all three.) For a few hours of each day, I deliberately cut myself off from both adults and my fellow teens; there was so much to process and figure out, and it seemed natural to withdraw into these ruminations while bicycling down to the harbor, or looking out from my bedroom window over the rooftops of my Brooklyn neighborhood. This kind of extended alone time, I now see as a parent of two teenage girls, is as outdated as a rotary telephone; in a world with the constant inputs of Facebook and texting and tweeting and IMing, no teen need be—can be—alone for more that a few minutes.

> Truth is, there were times in my teen years when I would have killed for the distraction of some online friends. But I don't envy the Facebook generation. Living in the blab-o-sphere, with a half-dozen open channels at all times, seems more like a burden than a pleasure, and the endless back-and-forth more an addiction than a choice. I know: I sound like a crotchety old Andy Rooney, scowling at this newfangled world from beneath the disapproving hedge of my eyebrows. But there is something to be said for looking for solace, and clues, inside your own being. Alone, you have no choice but to make friends with yourself; if you never manage that, your virtual friends won't do you much good.

In his editorial for the March 2, 2007 issue of the magazine *The Week*, editor William Falk addressed the value of "alone time." Explain his argument and discuss the extent to which you agree or disagree with his views. Support your position by referring to the passage and by providing reasons and examples from your own experiences, observations, or reading.

The following essays were then T-scored by fellow students. You'll find their scores in Appendix 7.

DC

Processing

In his editorial, William Falk uses a personal illustration to pursuade the new generation of teens to take some time to be alone on occasion. He describes the good his alone time did him when he was a teenager, then lamented the loss of that in the age of Twitter. His detailed description of his past experience helped illustrate the benefits fo his prescription.

While communication is vital to humanity, we do need space, on occasion, to develop as individuals. Humans are social creatures, but a constant barrage of input and networking prevents us from developing ideas of our own.

Even William Frank admits the quality of ones social life. In his illustration, he states that the reason he often brooded at the harbor was because he was "licking my latest social wound…mooning over Connie or Marie or Carole." Humans desire companionship. But more than that, its part of who we are. In an Isaac Asimov novel, a group of humans on a distant planet live in total isolation from each other. Because of this, they prevented the spread of diseases and were able to live longer. But as the novel reveals, the loss of companionship results in the loss of their humanity (their hearts, creativity, etc.). Without other people, there was nothing to remind them of what being human even ment.

But part of what it means to be human is to be an individual. This is something that can be largely lost on Twitter. One needs to be alone sometimes to establish unique though. Falk said it well, "There was so much to process and figure out." The human brain is essentially a computer. One important aspect of computers is that if you network them tightly enough, their programing and processing pathways merge into one super computer But the human race isn't supposed to be a super computor. It's our individuality that allows us to adapt and survive as a species. If there is one thing we have learned from studying life, its that homoginous groups die off once their environment changes; and our environment is almost constantly changing. Too much Twitter can be deadly.

Social Networking sites are not bad. They can be useful forms of communication; and communication is vital to humanity. But so is occasional isolation, so we can develop as separate entities. Both are necessary for our survival and sanity, so we must make sure we don't shut one down. Always remember to spend some time alone, and think about your experiences. Don't just be peebody7859, be you.

TC

Know Yourself

William Falk, in his editorial from The Week, argues that unless you understand yourself from time alone, no amount of friends will help you. He uses examples from his teenage years and compares them to those of his daughters to highlight the differences of values and urges that people need to be alone for thought.

It is true that among the noise of constant "Tweeting" we now have little time to explore in insides of our own minds rather than the minutae that others post online. Although a constant connection to friends is easy and nice due to the denial of problems it allows is is only when one is alone in the silence that one can tru-elly know one's self.

Perpetual connectivity to others allows one to completely ignore one's self and simply become one of many, a pod person or exact copy of all your friends. I have a younger brother who I have observed doing just that. His cell phone is glued alternatively to his ear or his fingertips, he hogs the computer, and keeps the TV and radio one even when not watching, in an effort to avoid himself. He is actu-ally afraid to even be alone. He might miss something. His friends might leave him behind. It is this that happens when one is never alone for reflections, no sense of self (or one only as one is part of a group). Solitude is required to define oneself.

Constant connectivity to others allow one to ignore problems that need to be solved. In Charles Dickens' classic novel A Tale of Two Cities, Sydney Canton is a failure of a man who (although he could be the best lawyer in London) spends his days carousing and drinking himself to an early grave. When he is with other people he accepts that his failure is something handed down by fate that he can not avoid. Only when he is alone does he know the truth: that all his misfortune is his own doing. It is from silence and solitude that we realize great truths about ourselves and our lives.

When one is alone one can not help but know one's self. There is no one else in that silence to speak to but yourself and to God. I like the author of the editorial. I value my alone time highly. It is the time when I can process the goings on of my day, my thoughts and feelings. It is the time when I know no one is watching so I can truelly be myself. It alows me to define myself by myself and not by a crowd of other people who dress, think, and talk exactly like me. It is in solitude that we can truelly be and know ourselves.

This age is full of people who can not free themselves to be themselves. They are constantly connected to their friends and some who are actually afraid to be alone. But they will never know who they truelly are apart from the crowd. They will never know their own strength or their own weakness. It is important that people realize how nessessary it is to be alone once in a will. We should remember to unplug periodically so we can remember that we exist.

NM

My mom graduated from high school in 1986. She had a great high school experience. My mom grew up to be a successful accountant and photographer. She is my idol, and when I was younger I used to say, "I want to be just like you when I grow up." As a child this is a wonderful dream. But now that I'm a little older I can understand that I will never be just like my mom. My mom and I grew up in different worlds, her generation and mine prove to be completely different. Although technology has brought many new advantages to our generation, it has removed the pleasures of the world, people, and experiences.

If we think about our lives without the internet or cell phones we laugh and think, "What would I do all day?" It's true. My homework would rarely be finished, because I couldn't recall off the top of my head when WWII started. Even just sitting around the house would be extra boring without checking Facebook, Myspace, and Twitter. Having a cell phone has changed our lives. We can be located or locate another person in seconds. A simple text can send information out faster than sound. Our generation must be brilliant, we control and navigate electronic devices like we were born doing it.

With this technology were does it leave us? Last week I was at the store and I bumped into a girl about my age who couldn't se me because her face was glued to the text she was sending. I quickly responded with "I'm sorry," looking at her face I felt her fear. It felt like she was scared to talk to me. I walked away thinking about this girl, then a question poped into my head. "She obviously had a lot to say in her text, so what made her incapeable of speaking words to me?" With cell phones and the internet, you today has lost the ability to communicate. Without the safety of our computer screen or the keypad on our phones, we do not share with the world our thoughts. Taking into consideration the advantages and faults of technology, todays youth need to move forward. Put down the cell phone for a day, and have a real live conversation. I'll bet it will prove to be eye opening.

LT

Sir Mixalot

Never before have the words "no man is an island" been truer than they are today. In today's world, cell phones and social networking sites have made us part of a huge network that we tap into nearly all the time. This kind of network, however, can be avoided in order to have time for quiet introspection. It is the fact of the matter that although being alone is important, social networking is a greater gift than a burden for happiness.

Being alone is something that I do often, and quite enjoy. On Sundays, I rarely see friends and spend the vast majority of the day at home or outside, taking walks or running. Throughout this time, I am alone. And when I am alone, I can think without the distractions of other people or necessary lip service to social rules. This time for me is much like that described by William Falk in his editorial. It is time for me to get to know myself better. For all people, this is time well spent. People who are quieter often seem to be smarter, more thoughtful, and kinder than those who are constantly with others. Perhaps this speaks to their personalities, but I think that it speaks to the power of alone time, and the introspection it allows. This introspection lets people get to know themselves. As William Falk tries to convince his audience in his editorial in The Week, if you can't be friends with yourself, having friends online isn't going to be much of a help. The Facebook generation, he argues, is tied down by the constant chatter and extended alone time is no longer possible. This is to their detriment.

I would partially disagree, however. As mentioned above, alone time is certainly a good thing. But having a vast social network is also a gift, and a non intrusive one as well. Being one's own friend is only half the battle, and the other half is having friends to share life with. Even though I spend time alone, I also mix it with a large dosage of time spent on Facebook. It is a window to the larger world that I can engage of disengage at my pleasure. If I don't want it to, it won't interfere with introspection. But it also serves as a portal to bring me closer to my friends.

Through its use, I can stay in touch with them on a more regular basis and make plans to meet. If anything, it enriches my life.

The question is not whether alone time or Facebook is more valuable, it is how they can be mixed in a way that works for the individual. In today's world, both are necessary to being happy and productive. One must know thine self, so that they can do what is right for them and make intelligent choices. They should also be with friends and use the tools given to them to accomplish this goal. In the end, people need to learn where to draw the line. For their own mental health, it is imperative that they do so.

TB

The Dissolution of Self

In his recent article for "The Week", William Falk argues that the constant interconnectedness that technology nurtures in today's youth has eradicated the benefits to be found from having real "alone time". Although the networking and awareness that the internet and cell phones enhance can be beneficial to teenagers, the lack of true relaxation and calmness harms our ability to focus and assert our individuality.

Modern technology allows for a much greater exchange of information than was ever available in the past. If we need help on homework, wish to stay informed about current events, or even just want to clarify the times that "The Hottub Time Machine" is playing at the local movie theater Saturday night, we can turn to Google and other such search engines. With just a click of a button, we can access the contents of countless libraries and news sources from the comfort of our own homes. Or, if just generic information seems too broad a target, we can look to our peers to gather opinions or info from everyday lives. However, this access to so much material and so many opportunities to talk to our friends can prove a dangerous distraction. Where thirty years ago, our parents had to work to procrastinate, with our updated resources, this natural instinct is much more easily accomplished. A simple question about due dates for an assignment can evolve into a lengthy discussion on movies, upcoming events, or various tidbits of juicy gossip. This amazing availiability of knowledge and communication can actually prevent learning and true interaction from ever having to happen.

When constantly surrounded by screens, text, and noise, our ability to accomplish a single, specific goal is greatly detrimented. The fact that we can listen to music, text, watch TV and do homework all at the same time doesn't mean we should. In Apple's commercials for their iPhone, they idolize the versatility of the product, basing its appeal on the fact that you can check your email, surf the web, and play games, all while still remaining on the phone. This access to so many options all the time pressures us to be constantly busy. Not only is this harmful when trying to do homework and juggle electronics at the same time, but this attitude hurts us in the way it carries over to real life as well. If we can't even allow ourselves to pick one goal and focus all of our energy on it for a period of time, then stepping back, relaxing, and detaching ourselves completely for a moment is completely out of the question. Without this focus and attention to detail, the quality of our work deteriorates and loses its meaning. No thought is put into it and thus we don't actually learn.

The hyperawareness of others that Facebook and the like encourage are just concentrated reflections of an already detrimental aspect of middle and high school. Although noticing one's surroundings and considering the impacts one's words have on others help one grow as a person, constantly worrying about what other people think can only harm us. My dad tells me that as a kid, he was self-conscious about his skinny wrists and ankles, and so he wore long pants and long-sleeved shirts for the entirety of seventh grade. This sounds ridiculous to me, but then I consider the minute facets of my appearance and personality that I obsess over, and it doesn't sound quite so far-fetched. But when school gets out and one is released from the shackles of this need for acceptance, time is finally allowed for true reflection. As Falk asserts, "there is something to be said for looking for solace, and clues inside your own being". But when I get home and soon after check my Facebook, I'm plugging myself back into this high school mentality without first stopping to collect my thoughts and consider myself. This allows for little to no time to discover the real me, instead shaping me by who others perceive me to be.

Technological advancement has provided our generation with access to so much more than our parents and grandparents had growing up. However, this bombardment of sights, sounds, and instant communication adds pressure to constantly multitask and leaves little time for reflection and thoughtful consideration. We must recognize our luck at having so much available to us, but at the same time, we must step back now and then to maintain our humanity.

Appendix 7: Scores of Sample Student Essays on a 30-minute ACT Prompt

These scores and the accompanying T-score commentary were generated by peer evaluators using the ACT 6-point rubric.

DC (high score)

1st reader

+	5	−
Good critical thinking Good vocabulary Strong point of view Few grammar errors		Progression of ideas would have been clearer if body paragraphs had begun with claims.

2nd reader

+	5	−
Good organization Good vocabulary Good examples		Could have been improved by less reliance on examples from the prompt and more original ones!

TC (medium score)

1st reader

+	3	−
Well-focused. Interesting vocabulary ("carousing"?)		Watch your pronouns; you switch between "you" and "one" a lot.

2nd reader

+	3	−
Clear viewpoint Good examples Nice structure		Some awkward grammar They/one/you? Pick one!

NM (low score)

1st reader

+	2	−
Good examples Good introduction Nice thesis		Need claims at the beginning of every paragraph. Need reference to the prompt or article. Use more non-personal examples.

2nd reader

+	1	–
Nice examples Nice flow Solid conclusion		Explain the connection between your examples and your thesis more.

LT (medium score)

1st reader

+	3	–
Has good sentence structure and great grammar Good use of language Nice introduction		I think you need to start the the third paragraph with a topic sentence because I was a bit lost. A bit unfocused.

2nd reader

+	3	–
Pretty good intro Sort of developed Not many grammar or spelling errors.		Either too unfocused or unorganized or both. I wasn't sure what you were saying.

TB (high score)

1st reader

+	5	−
Good vocabulary		Got a bit off topic in the first few paragraphs.
Good sentence structure		Be sure to restate the article.
Examples were great		
Clear position		

2nd reader

+	5	−
Fantastic thesis statement! Qualifies and solidifies position well.		Strive for interest-catching introduction.
Creative vocabulary		Be sure to start each paragraph with a claim.
Great progression of ideas		Add more to conclusion.
Effective variance in sentence structure.		

An Evaluative Annotated Bibliography

To Help You Understand Argument Construction

Bean, John C., et al. *Reading Rhetorically*. 2nd ed. New York: Langman, 2004. Print.

A great resource for improving your critical reading of nonfiction, this short text offers templates for writing various types of précis and shortcuts for offering concise summaries like the ones demanded of you on the ACT essay.

Lunsford, Andrea, et al. *Everything's An Argument*. 5th ed. New York: St. Martin's Press, 2010. Print.

A treasure trove of sample arguments for analysis, this college-level textbook provides excellent chapters on logically constructing and developing arguments. This latest edition also features a substantial section on rhetorical analysis. Includes readings from the Internet that coincide with discussion questions that can serve as on demand writing prompts.

To Assist with Your On Demand Writing

Angelillo, Janet. *Writing to the Prompt: When Students Don't Have a Choice*. Portsmouth, New Hampshire: Heinemann, 2005. Print.

This teacher text offers strategies for assisting students in writing on surprise prompts. It contains abundant samples of student work and how it was scored.

The College Board Online. 2005. "How the Essay Will Be Scored." July 26, 2007. Web.

The College Board offers its 6-point scoring rubric as well as reassurance that the intention is to "reward students for what they do well."

Marklein, Mary Beth. "ACT, SAT Essays Under the Red Pencil." *USA TODAY*. July 25, 2008. Web.
Openly cautioning students against plugging into the 5-paragraph essay formula, ACT essay readers confirm that even an essay with its thesis statement in the last line can qualify as having a clear position and demonstrate sophisticated facility of language.

To Help Improve Syntax and Style

Barzun, Jacques. *Simple and Direct: A Rhetoric for Writers*. 4th ed. New York: HarperCollins, 2001. Print.
As the title suggests, this text offers exercises and strategies for improving word economy. A perfect accompaniment to lessons in sentence modeling and "B.O.," this text features exercises inviting you to clean up the wordy syntax of sentences written by professional authors.

Williams, Joseph. *Style: Ten Lessons in Clarity and Grace*. San Francisco: Addison-Wesley, 2003. Print.
A college-level text that strives to make writers autonomous editors by taking them through self-diagnostic steps to isolate personal syntax problems.

Laying Claim to Your Topic Sentences Answer Key

1. __C__ Writing timed essays prepares us for college.

> While this may be the topic of this book, it is a debatable statement. Someone could write 2,000 timed essays and still not be prepared for college.

2. __O__ My cousin Peter had to write timed essays in all of his college classes.

> Yep, he did, but so what? Although this observation could be used as supporting evidence for the first claim, it is not a claim.

3. __C__ Writing well under time constraints has benefits that extend beyond college.

> This is debatable. A sculptor who earned a BA may never have to write under time constraints after graduation.

4. __O__ Timed essays do not necessarily have 5 paragraphs.

> This is an honest observation and therefore not debatable. In fact, I'm willing to bet that some low-scoring timed essays have consisted of as little as one paragraph.

5. __C__ What matters most in a timed essay are specific supporting details.

> This is a claim because, while it sounds reasonable, it remains debatable whether specific supporting details matter MOST. I could contend that writing legibly matters more.

6. __C__ The more timed essays you write, the more fun they become!

> Of course, I'd like you to believe that this is a fact, but it is (sadly) a debatable statement.